ARISE

ARISE

A Revolution in Natural Divinity

LIZETE MORAIS

Copyright ©2025 by Lizete Morais. All rights reserved.

No part of this book may be reproduced or used in any manner without the prior written permission of the copyright owner, except for the use of brief quotations in a book review. To request permissions, contact publisher@worldchangers.media.

Disclaimer: This is a work of nonfiction. Nonetheless, some of the names and identifying character traits of people featured in the stories herein have been changed in order to protect their identities. Any resulting resemblance to persons either living or dead is entirely coincidental.

The publisher and the Author make no representations or warranties of any kind with respect to this book or its contents, and assume no responsibility for errors, inaccuracies, omissions, or any other inconsistencies herein. The content of this book is for informational purposes only and is not intended to diagnose, treat, cure, or prevent any condition or disease, including mental health conditions. You understand that this book is not intended as a substitute for consultation with a licensed healthcare provider. The use of this book implies your acceptance of this disclaimer.

At the time of publication, the URLs displayed in this book refer to existing websites owned by Lizete Morais and/or the authors' affiliates. WorldChangers Media is not responsible for, nor should be deemed to endorse or recommend, these websites; nor is it responsible for any website content other than its own, or any content available on the internet not created by WorldChangers Media.

Paperback ISBN: 978-1-955811-88-0
E-book ISBN: 978-1-955811-89-7

First paperback edition: July 2025

Author photo: Lizete Morais
Cover artwork: @ MdRaselMahmud via AdobeStock
Interior artwork: @MariMuz via AdobeStock
Cover design, layout, and typesetting: Bryna Haynes
Editors: Audra Figgins, Bryna Haynes

Published by WorldChangers Media
PO Box 83, Foster, RI 02825
www.WorldChangers.Media

This book is dedicated to every person and every thing that has ever loved me.

You have been my master teachers in the only essence that multiplies itself the more it is given away.

You will always be my personal heroes, and I will love you until my eternal end.

CONTENTS

Introduction: Can Women Have It All? 1

(Interlude) 13

Chapter One — Initiation: Awakening to Authenticity 15

PART I: AWARENESS

The True Power of Transformation 23

(Divinity Whispers) 33

Chapter Two — Clarity: Accessing the Crystalline Within 35

Chapter Three — Calling: The Attitude of Purpose 57

(A Call to Return Home) 71

Chapter Four — Confidence: The Natural Power of You 75

PART II: ACTIVATION

The Heart of Alchemy and Sacred Service 87

(Divinity Whispers) 99

Chapter Five — Courage: Stepping into the Unknown 101

(Lion's Gate Transmission) 121

Chapter Six — Charisma: The Art of Living and Loving as You 123

Chapter Seven — Connection: The Tribe Supporting Your Legacy 141

PART III: ALIGNMENT

The Power of Your Light and Accepting All Is Right   159

(Divinity Whispers)   175

Chapter Eight — Consciousness: The Cornerstone of Creation   177

(Year of the Dragon Initiation)   195

Chapter Nine — Congruence: Everything is Momentum   199

Chapter Ten —Compassion: The Leadership of Christed Consciousness   223

(A Line in the Sand)   247

PART IV: ARISE

Unlocking Legacy   249

Chapter Eleven —Welcome to Everyday Eden   253

(Year of the Snake Initiation)   271

Chapter Twelve — Co-Creating in the New World   273

Resources   285

Recommended Reading   286

Acknowledgments   287

About the Author   289

About the Publisher   291

Arise

A Revolution in Natural Divinity

INTRODUCTION

Can Women Have It All?

Welcome, dear one, to this journey and to these sacred pages. We are traveling through time and space as students and masters of this great mystery of life, and I am honored to share this story, this journey, and these soul secrets with you.

Writing this book and exposing what I have discovered is the single most significant and scary step I have taken yet, and I do it with all reverence and humility as the next step I must take in this ongoing evolution. We are in tremendous times, and each one of us is elevating into the version of us we came to embody. My highest hope is that this book may be of support in the journey of your becoming.

May I be so bold as to assume that you, like me, are a seeker? Yes? I am also a leader, a lover, a creator, and an artist. A human soul that has dreams, gifts, talents, needs, desires, and wishes. It is wonderful to meet you here. I have been collecting these sacred pieces of the puzzle I now present to you in the form of this book. A journey I have called *ARISE: A Revolution in Natural Divinity*.

Though this is a pathway for you learn and tools to help you forge your own journey, this book also shares my personal story and how I came to put this puzzle together. I focus on the period between June 2021 through January 2025. At the beginning of this period, my world as I had known it had collapsed, echoing what was going on in the wider world. We were still at the height of the Covid-19 pandemic, experiencing chaos, exhaustion, and disarray. My best friend, partner, and fiancé, whom I call Nathan in this book, had just melted down our relationship—the main relationship I depended on for shelter, food, and survival. I was in the middle of the Costa Rican jungle in an off-grid wooden house we'd built together.

It was a wake-up call of the direst kind. With two hundred euros to my name, I got on a flight to Portugal, going home to my mother. I had invested everything into my relationship with Nathan, and its dissolution pushed me off a cliff where it felt I had broken in a million pieces as my ego hit the earth. I was devastated, but with space and time, I realized that what shattered was indeed only ego: the idea about who I believed I needed to be in order to be loved. I lost all desire to be someone I was not. I recognized that my conditioning and biases—all that "training" and "intelligence"—had led to this miserable result. Now, everything was up for question. I didn't know who to trust or what would happen next. It was terrifying, but it was also truth. And it set me free.

From this place of not knowing and rock bottom, I could only listen. I didn't have any other option. I just began listening, and in that still place, guidance came. Things started working out. Opportunities opened up. People appeared just when I needed them. What I learned is so revolutionary—the complete opposite of what I was trained to believe my whole life—and yet, the results are undeniable.

FINDING OUR NATURAL DIVINITY

In just three and a half years, three major things transformed in my everyday experience and waking everyday reality:

- I have completed this book, building a whole new method of transformation. I have dreamed since I was a little girl to be able to make a contribution to my fellow human travelers. I wanted to find my authentic voice and help others heal, and through the tools, insights, and understanding I gained on this journey, that is now more than a possibility.

- I have transformed my body by losing thirty kilos with no sacrifice or diet, only a transformation in the perspective of and relationship to my physical body. Through what I will teach you in this process, you, too, can access your vital and youthful energy through memory in the cells.

- I have built the ARISE Academy: The Home of Multidimensional Mastery. Through it, I provide tools, training, transmissions, and teaching about understanding and expanding consciousness. This is the Earth School I wish I had gone to, and I hope it will be a part of my legacy, something I will continue to develop for the rest of my mortal life. Not only am I helping others through this work, but I have also found my purpose and given myself a job.

- I've established a strong foundation and created security for myself using the gifts that come innately and naturally to me. My multidimensional gifts came online, allowing me to create the most incredible experiences for my clients on retreats, sing the most beautiful songs, and watch as the frequency of love and healing sets all things back into alignment and agreement with divinity.

I didn't achieve these things by following the ways I had been trained or programmed to believe reality works. I was at a place where I no longer had the need to survive. So I surrendered. By releasing my need to know the answers, silence entered, along with original thought and intelligence. This was the start of my training to be guided by my higher consciousness.

Our natural divinity is being reconnected to our higher dimensional self. This self is outside of time and sees the full picture of existence. It holds the multidimensional gifts of creation and knows itself as eternal. This is the wisdom we need for our own internal development, for our personal relationships with family and friends, and for our unique skills and talents that we are meant to share with the greater whole. Especially as women, this can be challenging because of the weight of expectations and responsibilities.

Can women truly have it all? I wondered this for myself, for all fellow women, and on behalf of humanity. But what does it mean for a woman to have it all? For me now, it means that I need to be secure in my relationships with myself, with Spirit, and with others. Within these pages, I share my personal experience of becoming crystalline clear for myself. When we are anchored in energy, intention, focus, and devotion, we live in the present, the now moment, which is where we can create for the future we want to have.

What does having it all mean to you, dear one? Is it a beautiful home in your favorite place in the world? The perfect partner? The body and health you've always dreamed of? Is it a certain lifestyle? Are you raising children, or giving your love to pets and others? Are you investing in your own creativity?

When a woman benefits, is supported, and wins, everyone wins. It is her truest nature. Whether you are a woman looking to truly live her potential and purpose, or you are a person looking to be a blessing in a woman's life and share that abundant life in harmony with her, we are about to embark on the journey to tap into your incredible natural divine intelligence. To have it all, we must embody our natural divinity. This is the only real superpower. My goal is to help you align so deeply with the truest and most divine part of yourself, refine the essence of your gifts, and ultimately manifest your truest desire.

Whatever you imagine or envisage for yourself, dear one, I hope that you truly get it and more. However, even more than this, I hope you will find and learn, through these pages and this path, that you—right here and now—are the essence, the inspiration, the imagination, and the power that gets to enjoy all of that creation. Indeed, that creation is *waiting* for you to embody your whole self. You have everything you need; it's already within you.

One of the most inspiring insights gleaned from one of my first mentors of consciousness, Rikka Zimmerman, was that in just one generation we could change the world if mothers (including mother figures like aunties, godmothers, grandmothers, and community leaders) could raise their children in love and security. Imagine that! With what I've experienced these last few years, I believe this is true.

Women. Mothers. Lovers. Leaders.

We are the solution and the leaders we have been waiting for. So why isn't it happening on a large scale yet? So many of us feel depleted, defeated, destitute, and depressed—we're being held back by four major issues, or shadows:

- **Self-Doubt:** We are not clear on what we want—and even when we are, the majority of us are told it is impossible. We second-guess our intuition, and are not confident in the steps we are taking.

- **Self-Sacrifice:** We have not been nurtured to believe in our innate power and authority to create. As we have not been raised in our natural power, we hold many subconscious and unconscious beliefs and story patterns ensuring the repetition of cycles of settling and suffering.

- **Self-Sabotage:** We have been made to fear our thoughts, our desires, and our power. When we can't see opportunity or fear failure or the unknown, there are so many ways we sabotage ourselves. As we can't see these sneaky patterns, we can't self-correct, and tend to repeat the same cycles.

- **Self-Pity:** We have deliberately not been taught how to transform any of it. We are caught in the loop of blaming and shaming others for the situations we find ourselves in.

If you feel stuck, if you are unsure why you keep investing in things to only have the rug pulled out from under you, if you feel powerless to make changes in your life because you believe you have no other choice—believe again. If you are a human being, you have the power of divinity within you. The answers are within you if you will accept what the stillness and whisper of your higher self is saying. I hope the pathway this book offers will illuminate how to do just that.

THE ESSENTIAL ECOSYSTEM OF EVERYDAY EDEN

The Essential Ecosystem of Everyday Eden is channeled work I received and walked consciously for the last four years. It is a roadmap to unlock your authenticity, to operate through time and space as a sovereign being as you discover your essence is indeed co-creating your reality. Who you are as a person and what you can do with your choice is what defines freedom. And that is my only agenda.

Through the Essential Ecosystem, I clearly sense and activate the guidance of the Holy Spirit, the Spirit of Wholeness. It supports the righteousness or the right standing with our Christed Consciousness. Its most priceless output is crystalline clarity.

The Essential Ecosystem forms the journey to wholeness. It is based on the foundation of these three pillars, each of which contain three building blocks:

- **Awareness:** The soil of our subconscious mind as we dive deep into the unseen and energetic realms of our creating consciousness. Building CLARITY around our CALLING and healing the inner conviction that produces our incorruptible CONFIDENCE.

- **Activation:** The powerful primordial waters spring back to life to regenerate our cellular structure as we enter into deeper energetic harmony with our source. Conjuring the COURAGE of the heart to authentically express our natural CHARISMA that magnetizes the CONNECTIONS needed for your unique calling.

- **Alignment:** The light of truth that keeps us balanced and stable through a world of duality. Nurturing and cultivating the CONSCIOUSNESS that serves us as a guiding light. To remain COHERENT in the ways of COMPASSION and Christed Consciousness.

When we put these nine steps and three pillars together, we ARISE. Going on this adventure will stabilize you as you discover a higher consciousness and higher perspective for your life, love, and leadership. My own journey on this path has been a revolution, a lifeline that has brought me to *this* moment of manifesting *these* words. I began on my mother's floor in heartbreak, but have since come to know who I am and trust who I am from the inside out. You too, beloved, are always meant to rise from the ashes. Your authenticity, your Christed seed self, was created before the world began. We call on this seed now to be planted in fertile soil. Receive the waters that bring it to life and let it rise into the light of your understanding. To have it all, we have to be our whole self.

The results I found with the Essential Ecosystem have been replicated in other clients, students, and friends who have done this work with me in the different containers I have created in person and online. The beauty of this is that it's an ongoing process; I feel I am only just getting started. I'm far from perfected, and yet so perfectly at peace with how far I have come and ready for what comes next. The greatest gift I have received is the connection to my higher self, and I now extend that invitation to you to connect with yours more effortlessly. Your higher self has all the answers you will ever need. I can serve only as an example. It is an ongoing evolution, and I meet you here as a fellow master and student of this journey of wholeness.

Step by step, we will review experiences, frameworks, and the wisdom shared from these lessons for you to try on for size. What you believe affects your life and yours alone. Mine affects mine. I can never, nor will I ever, try to convince you of anything. Please take what serves you and leave the rest for those who may resonate.

Women can have it all because we are deeply connected to all, and we are co-creating and regenerating with Mother Earth and

Father God. We can share it all with our beloved men and brothers. Walking in peace and harmony allows us to not only live a great life, but to create our legacy of leadership.

One of peace. One of love. One of security.

COMING HOME

Sometime during 2008, I was traveling home from a business trip to the Netherlands, where I was based. I can't recall exactly which trip, as travel was frequent in those days in my role as a corporate trainer and leadership development manager. I was exhausted, and knew there were only a few more hours left to journey. I got up from my seat and made my way to the bathroom. Passing the many rows of passengers, a sigh released in my body as I whispered, "Almost home," in an attempt to lift myself up. Right in the middle of the aisle, I heard a clear voice say, *"You will learn that you are always home. Home is right in your own body."*

I have had thousands of conversations with people from every single walk of life since 2006 when I started my coaching practice. Each person comes in with a unique problem, situation, and set of circumstances. Yet each client has a universal desire. They long to be safe and sound. The human being hopes, more than anything, to be safe and sound. This is the foundation for every good and wonderful thing that life has to offer. And repeatedly, I found this thread in others and in myself.

My highest hope is that this book is a homecoming for you. Home: the ultimate human word. The place that signifies deep comfort and solace. The space that offers nurturing and stability. The sanctuary of love and laughter that calls the soul to delight and rest and make love. Home.

So, here is the biggest question that we are going to solve during our time together, through this journey and in this book: if the priority of every human being, every parent, every lover, every pet owner, every leader is to be safe and sound, how on earth have we ended up with this war-torn, destitute, unfair, and dysfunctional world? Is this the best we can do? I think not!

I know that this is the most universal need not only because of my research and my personal observation, but because it is also the highest reason that every government, political party, and world authority uses to motivate any action or justify any restriction. This may sound familiar. It is for the safety of the people, right? So, we all agree that the safety of people is the highest priority of all leadership of humanity everywhere.

We as humanity need better leaders. In every single arena. In every single community. This book is for these leaders. This wisdom and teachings are for those who are called to be a new breed of power. The power of love, the power of unity, the power of life. The naturally divine human who understands that safety and being safe space is the highest possible ambition of both love and power. My work is about mapping out the exact divine blueprint for the leaders that we have been waiting for. That leader is you.

Welcome to the revolution. Welcome to the journey where our evolution is revealed. In essence, this is truly my deepest heart's desire for your journey, dear reader. Although we cover theory, I am offering frameworks to enhance understanding and explain the different phenomena I have discovered in my research. This ancient and futuristic wisdom that I want to share with you cannot be shared in the traditional way of teaching. It is already inside of you. I cannot tell you truth because your soul already knows all truth. I can only create the container in which you can experience it for yourself. I can only guide you down the hallways and point out the ancient writing on the wall that you may have missed or not have seen quite in this way before.

I always thought and hoped I would be "somebody"—that I would do something of some significance in the world. I didn't know how I was going to do this, but there was always a sense from my earliest of knowings that I was here for a reason. A purpose. At this moment of my life, I know exactly what that purpose is.

Part of realizing this purpose is this very book you hold now in your hands. Thank you for being part of my journey, and I hope that the pages you hold become a powerful key that opens a mystical and majestic door that can never be closed. A portal into the heart of what it means to be alive, to be human, to be free, and to be home. To live your legacy as I now live mine.

I do not say these words lightly. In truth, I don't say any words lightly. Words create worlds—truly. The words that follow are some of the most important I will ever share. We are in for a wonderful adventure, dear one, and I'm delighted you're joining me. I have held on to these memories, these mysteries buried deep in my soul, and now I will share them with you. These are sacred tales. A revolution of natural divinity and the path that lead me to remember a frequency, a song, a dream, and a hope I call Everyday Eden.

When I imagine Everyday Eden, I imagine us returning home. To a garden, to a kitchen, to a warm blanket. To a place we can snuggle in and get comfortable, on retreat. Here we can take a breath and feel our heart stir as we remember. Home. As we remember Eden. As we remember a higher dream that is asking to be birthed into reality once again. One where all can be safe and sound.

I'm so excited for you to join me on this adventure, for us to come home together.

(INTERLUDE)

The teachers of teachers,
the leaders of leaders,
the masters of masters are rising.

But they walk differently than what we have seen before.
They come with no accolades, no titles, no attachment to approval.
They sell themselves at no cost,
and they have no pretense that life
has treated them differently or better than anyone else.

They will teach by their very vibration.

Their presence will emanate,
and in an instant with their gaze
they will pierce the darkness with pure benevolence.
They will teach only by example and story,
as they will have learned that all dogma is dead.

No theory or framework.
No obedience to the steps will rescue them.

They will have been illuminated,
that each Sacred Soul of humanity,
is a divine precious and beloved child of the universe.
Beyond any material possession.

That each of us walks a unique
and blessed journey
where no one is higher or lower
than any another.
There is no separation in them.

These teachers, these prophets of peace,
walk in humility, purity, and imperfection.
They have healed the shame that kept them small,
and stuck, and suffocated.

They know they can save no one ...
but instead create safe spaces for all
to find their own light within.
Then each will know,
we are all sons and daughters of LIFE.

Mother Earth is waiting in trembling anticipation of
the sons and daughters who will remember that we are HERE!

It is time to ARISE.

CHAPTER ONE

Initiation: Awakening to Authenticity

A beautiful, multi-colored, wooden cabin sat nestled in the jungle, surrounded by an immense green landscape and an explosion of life. It took my breath away as I stepped out of the car, taking it all in. It was January 13, 2019, and for the next five days and nights, I would be living in this beautiful setting in Cancun, Mexico, with a goal to reconnect. I was not clear as to what I would be reconnecting with just yet, but I knew I had been guided to this very spot and moment.

I turned to my beautiful guide, Sky. She was delighted at my reaction, her bright eyes twinkling.

Sky had rented this place for me and was going to serve as my guide on this private retreat. We had met at an author's conference in Las Vegas a few years before and stayed in touch ever since. She had the air of another world about her, but was the most direct and truthful person I had ever met, and something deep in my soul resonated with her. "I need to heal my confidence," I had told her. I was tired of feeling my potential slip away from me, like an endless void that never settled. I was being called to end the separation, even though it was not clear what I was separate from.

We walked onto the deck—the perfect setting for morning coffee in the jungle—and then into the cabin. The inside was inviting and simple. A four-poster bed draped by a wispy, white mosquito net served as the centerpiece. Besides the main living space with a few wooden pieces of furniture, there was a simple kitchen and bathroom with running water. It would do just fine.

"You will be sleeping here tonight," Sky said, and I suddenly realized what that meant: sleeping alone in the jungle—in Mexico. Familiar fear crept in my blood, turning me cold.

"You'll be fine, dear one," she said, seemingly reading my mind and sensing my resistance.

Retreats can be like a portal where you step into another time and space. This is an unknown place of opportunity where the habitual narrative doesn't exist, and the programmed conditioning doesn't apply. Stepping into this jungle was the exact medicine I needed.

For the next three days, we began early with deep meditation and then ventured into the jungle, the unexplored territory serving as the cocoon and container for major revelations and breakthroughs. I was starting to understand my fear. As my perspective shifted and my consciousness elevated, the jungle came alive. The beauty of the natural world washed over me in relentless and seemingly eternal waves.

By the fourth morning, the jungle was more familiar; I trusted my footing as I walked down the dirt tracks to the cenotes. These natural underground lakes of pure, clear water were breathtaking. I slipped into one, feeling the water support and awaken my energetic body with its frequency and warm embrace. After my invigorating swim, we were walking peacefully back to the cabin when suddenly a deep fear flooded my system, turning my blood ice cold.

A life-sized rock sculpture with three enormous snakes had come into view. There were other sculptures of men, women, children, and other animals nearby, but this one gripped me, and I couldn't tear my eyes away. Sky, being the excellent guide she is, knew that this was the moment we were waiting for.

She gently took my hand and asked, "Are you afraid?"

I nodded silently.

"Of a rock?"

I shook my head, words still escaping me. I pointed at the snakes, my arm shaking. I was deathly afraid of snakes. Even just the image of them.

"Do you want your potential?" Sky asked.

I nodded again, feeling a little silly and self-conscious. I had come a long way to unlock my personal power in both years and distance, and this was the key moment to claim it back.

"If you want your power, you must conquer your fear."

I knew it was the truth. Turning away from her, with a tremble in my step, I walked toward the stone. I stood before it and bowed my head whispering, "Please, Holy Spirit, guide me as always." I struggled to breathe as I looked up at the snakes.

Peace instantly filled my system like a warm trickle, the old icy fear slipping out of my veins. I could feel the snakes and see them. They were moving in another dimension. And just like that, they started speaking. I could hear three loud and distinct voices, speaking all at the same time, yet I could understand them all. It was not just words they communicated; I felt their very emotion and presence as they spoke to me. They each had a singular message.

The first snake was sharing deep anguish. It was distraught at the separation between my kind (womankind and humankind) and its kind. It was completely aware of itself, and our separation felt ancient. It longed for us to become reacquainted.

The second snake shared so much love and whispered, "Do not be afraid of who and what you are." It opened itself up and I could feel a tremendous vital life force.

The third one said calmly and confidently, "I will show you the path back to the Garden."

I wept. For how many eons had I been separated, afraid and helpless to find where I belonged? I felt pain rip through my body. How many thousands of years had my soul not wept and wailed with these exact questions? I let out a visceral cry as I felt my heart explode open. It was a sound I had never heard before—I wasn't even aware a sound like that could come from my body. At first primal and ancient, like a wounded animal, fear, distress, panic, and terror released and were transformed into bellowing laughter of relief, joy, and unbridled delight.

A CONSCIOUS INITIATION

Anyone watching would have called me nuts, and maybe you think that now. In truth, this was the first moment I was truly alive.

While in eastern civilizations the snake is revered as a symbol of life force or the kundalini, our spark of the divine, that was not the side I had been raised on. Snakes in the western world are painted as evil, dangerous, and poisonous. In the Christian teachings I grew up with, snakes are synonymous with the devil. This was compounded by the fact that I had spent my first sixteen years in Botswana, Southern Africa, where I was warned against snakes by everyone every time I ventured into the bush.

But this moment went against all that. It was an initiation. A moment where the Earth, the stars, and the universe aligned to create a significant shift in my awareness. This shift created an activation of my very DNA so that I could walk in greater alignment with my true purpose. I have had multiple out-of-body experiences in my life, and supernatural occurrences are not uncommon for me, but this was the origin story of the Essential Ecosystem for Everyday Eden.

It is not that all of a sudden, we become superhuman with this kind of consciousness expansion; instead, we realize that being a regular human is the most absolutely divine experience that could possibly be imagined. Death is what the snake has come to represent in many cultures, but it also represents the end of the fear of death as we realize we are eternal.

This is a key in our adventure, dear reader. When there is a true understanding of our eternity, there can be nothing but peace. There is nothing but time to do, explore, investigate, and enjoy. However, as a human mortal, I am constantly told that I have to hurry, that time is running out. The understanding of the power of the sacred snake symbol does not nor could ever replace "the singular source of all creation" (what some call God); however, it empowers us to know divine will. To know the divine will as free will for myself is the key that unlocks the door of natural divinity. Understanding how our bodies are created and work in harmony with the laws of divinity is how we learn to walk in agreement.

This may feel confusing to you now. I completely understand that it might not feel like a living miracle just to be alive. It was only at what felt like the endless, ripe old age of forty-two that I understood this, and it's a revelation that turned my life around. Ready?

Life doesn't give you what you want. It shows you who you are being.

To break this down even further, to me, "being" means what you believe, accept, and allow. What we subconsciously and unconsciously think, feel, and know about ourselves is dictating what we receive, what we tolerate, and what we choose to allow.

Now, with this knowing, how do you feel about being alive? This is the beginning of cultivating elevated awareness. You are no longer reacting to your environment; you are co-creating. You are learning to observe, to take everything as a lesson with humble acceptance.

You are alert and awake, enjoying the experience of your life with a higher sensitivity. Your enjoyment, fulfillment, and temperament become more neutral. You turn all the lead you were given into absolute gold.

Our natural divinity is bringing the actual power of God, creation, and natural divinity into every moment through free will. It is the vast universe of potential I felt within me as apathy, grief, shame, and guilt my whole life. And for what? For being human? For making mistakes? No. I carried these things because I had chosen to know good and evil. I had said yes to the snake. Yes, indeed I am referring to the same story of our creation—the one we have heard for eons as recorded in the Bible's book of Genesis.

Regardless of your personal faith or inclination, the story of our origin affects our perception as a collective of who we understand ourselves to be. This is how far I have journeyed through time and cellular remembrance to know what I now share with you. We separated from the Creator and the garden because we were given the gift of free will. We alone would know good and evil and have the opportunity to judge for ourselves. When we live the consequences of our choices, we question our ability, our intelligence, our worthiness, and even our identity. What is the use of free will if I'm only going to create chaos?

Well, that is the very reason we need to build multidimensional mastery. To have peace with God and with ourselves, and to choose anew. To choose life and life more abundantly. To not be fooled by the form or the appearance of a thing, but to know its essence as we choose with wisdom. This process and this journey are all about right standing with our truest essence, which was designed in the image and likeness of the one we call God. That likeness and nature is pure, unconditional love.

We all know this story, and that is the only story that truly needs to be set straight. Natural divinity is the return of Everyday Eden. Alignment with the supreme consciousness will reveal how humanity knows the difference between right and wrong, good and evil. That it does not utter the word love while it stabs the other with pure hate and jealousy.

Peace with God. Each in their own soul. That is all each is responsible for. When each one does this for themselves, we will know peace. Because we all agree on one thing: God is love. All that is left is that we act like it.

Let's march on, warrior.

PART I: AWARENESS

The True Power of Transformation

For every master on the journey there comes a moment of acceptance that there will always be the known, the unknown, and the unknowable. This is the moment wisdom begins.

My five-day retreat in the jungle was over, but there was one last thing we needed to do. With a last glance, a sigh of relief, and a wave of deep gratitude, we headed to Cancun. I had realized that what I truly love is the Earth. This beautiful, abundant, magnificent planet. Mars has its place, but our Mother—wow, had my eyes and ears been opened. "Eyes to see and ears to hear" indeed had taken on a whole new meaning. I had spent over twenty-two years in a Christian church as a student of the word of God, and yet I had never really noticed the feminine side of this incredible creation: the Garden.

Next up, Sky had organized something special. We were going to Tulum to visit the Mayan Temples, and this would not be an ordinary visit. We were going under the cover of night and would watch the sunrise. It sounded nice enough, but I was not very excited. In truth, I was already peeking ahead and longing for the next leg of my trip, which would be to Costa Rica to visit a new special friend.

I knew nothing about these ancient ruins or about the Mayans, except the rumors that they performed human sacrifice back in the day; it sounded very macabre to me. How could I even ask for more after such a retreat, anyway? I was already so happy with everything I'd received. What could possibly add to this experience? All these questions raced through my mind until we got there.

Walking up the path to the temples, I could sense a shift in vibration. Giggling, excited, and a little nervous navigating in the dark, we entered the unknown. I had stepped onto sacred ground, and I felt it. We became more serious and aware, the atmosphere of the night making itself known, the air lighter and more intense at the same time. I entered another dimension, and it was tangible. I looked up to see Venus shining bright in the night sky, and there, under a clear dome of black velvet, the temples stood, light seeming to emanate from inside them even though there were no lights on. They were majestic and tears suddenly filled my eyes and rolled gently down my cheeks. It was a coming home of sorts that felt misplaced.

I reached the foot of the temple and started running up the stairs. Yes, running. If you know me at all, you know I don't run anywhere. But there I was, taking leaps and bounds in the dark up the tall steps. I was fearless. Arriving at the top of the temple, I stretched out my hands and raised my arms to the heavens. I felt I had done this thousands of times before. In another time, I had served here, I remembered. A message in English, in tongues, and in another language poured out of my being. My soul was finding its voice from knowledge long forgotten.

I remembered specifically talking to the elements, blessing them, and praying for peace. I spoke of empowerment, unity, and the rise of a people who did not compromise their brother or sister. It felt like the ancient past meeting the expansive future.

Genesis.

I watched the sunrise standing on that temple dome. The night relented her grasp; the veil lifted, and the remnants of the stars faded from view. I saw the sea. Wide and strong, in and out. I felt the wind blow and kiss my cheek. Someone was in the wind. Mother. The Great Night. Air. Water. Earth. Fire. I saw the building blocks of life. The basis of all alchemy. I saw the truth of the cross, the Christed path to follow the fourth-dimensional awareness. Divinity and natural law side by side. It was quite an incredible sunrise.

When I was ready, I found Sky at the bottom of the steps, and we walked back through the park. I was reborn. I remembered who I was in a whole new way. Our hug goodbye was and is endless, as I will forever be grateful for this living angel and guide in my life. The taxi ride to the airport was emotional and tearful as I watched the scenery whisk by.

The mood shifted swiftly upon reaching the airport. The busyness and multitude of people was suddenly overwhelming—I was, for the first time, noticing the shift in frequency from the natural world to the fabricated world.

I had stepped into *awareness*.

STABILITY LEADS US TO OURSELVES

Awareness is where our journey begins. It is simply paying attention to all the information at hand with all the senses we have available. I consider awareness as a muscle of consciousness that you exercise in order to discern what is real, and this is the first pillar of our Essential Ecosystem.

Awareness is the spiritual power and the strength we use to organize our consciousness through time and space. As we expand and exercise this ability, we are able to not only see just two sides to every story but a third. We can reflect and see patterns clearly. This is how we can observe ourselves and the other. This is what we need to do to love God and each other. So, let us lay the very first foundation of this powerful and life-changing understanding.

I remember walking to the train station one dark and rainy night in the Netherlands. I was a training and talent development executive working in corporate America, and had just completed a presentation for a leadership team around the talent development program in one of the facilities I was responsible for. All of a sudden, I started having a mind conversation that may feel familiar to you.

You could have done better! You know you did better last night! You always blow it—so-and-so looked so bored. Why were you so nervous about that part of the presentation?

Woulda. Coulda. Shoulda. I was drowning in it when a thought I'd never had before came to me.

Why can't I just be the Lizete I know I am inside?

What a profound question. Why can't we just be ourselves, as we are inside? It should be the most natural and effortless thing. Yet we are the great mystery, dear one. To ourselves and others in so many ways. I hope to serve as a sister for you, and share the wisdom and revelation I've received, for every step of this journey. Within the Essential Ecosystem, we are bringing ourselves into more and more alignment with who we truly are. That one inside. The higher self. The one who knows. The one who longs to create a life of love!

Awareness was, for a long time, held in the hands of spiritual and religious wisdom. No one living in the "real world" had time to consider these lofty concepts. Yet the research I will share around this topic concerning the Essential Ecosystem has changed that perspective entirely. Awareness is for everyone, as it is exactly how reality is co-created. Through our consciousness, we co-create with the divinity within us in every present moment. Everyone has the power of choice, and yet we live in a world that encourages using coping mechanisms outside of ourselves.

Our liberation is our thoughts, feelings, judgments, and actions. As we take accountability and authority over our lives, we come that much closer to living our authenticity. We only need to take the time to listen and observe. To be aware. Just how many times have you said the dreaded words, "Oh, I didn't see that coming"? This is where it turns around.

To know what is real and begin walking in our personal truth is to experience what we want to see and what is really happening at the same time. While aware of all the discrepancies, we use default behaviors and actions that delightfully sweep truth under the rug. When we want something to be true, it might be, but it also might not be. Awareness offers the ability to cultivate the neutrality that we are willing to hold on and willing to let go at any moment. This seems impossible until we decide to seek truth above every convenience. It is not an easy path to take, but I have found that it is the path of least pain.

To activate the power of awareness and cultivate the frequency of Everyday Eden, we begin with an understanding of time. It is important to understand that wherever and whenever we find these words, we are here. We are always right here and right now. There is also a past that informs every molecule, atom, and cell that has created everything up to this moment of now. Likewise, we intuitively know that there is a sequence of time we are still facing, which we call the future. But the only power and ability we hold is in the here and now. It sounds like I am stating the obvious and yet, when we truly stop and understand this common sense, we unlock our true power.

In many dark moments when I was on my knees and in despair seeking answers, higher guidance would say one thing: Remember who you are! That never sounded like much of a solution to me until I understood the concept of time this way.

Our choice and free will, in the here and now, are the most powerful resources we have. When we are not using awareness consciously, we react to circumstances as if they are singular events occurring at random. But when we awaken to conscious awareness, we create our circumstances. As we step into the power of consciousness, consider the words reaction and creation. If you move one letter, one becomes the other. And this similarity continues with their meaning: The former is an act of survival while the latter is an act of divine alignment.

The mastery of our awareness, what we perceive, has the power to support us and become the source of our own stability. I call this Christed Consciousness, the power to connect to the Christed, to have unified and divine intuitive knowing within our own being. What a delightful thought, being the source of your own stability! It does not mean you will not share your life and experience with others; actually, it is quite the opposite. The more stable you are mentally, emotionally, physically, and energetically, the better your experience of life, the more life-giving your collaborations, and the greater the results of your co-creation.

Stability is necessary for any great work. This doesn't mean that every aspect of life is ideal or in the perfect state right now, but it means that we have the mental, emotional, and physical energy and circumstances to be peacefully working with a clear mind to its resolution. Financial stability is also important so that we can move in the world with greater freedom and flexibility. So please don't be gaslit by those who make you feel selfish for craving stability. I did this for what felt like eons, a result of a wound of deep unworthiness and abandonment. Stability is key to realize the call in your soul, so don't fear to own your dreams or drive. Mastering your awareness is the fastest way to discern what is real, what is good, and what is true, which will support you in every direction you choose to walk in.

To cultivate stability in everyday life, we require three things, which are the three facets of awareness:

- **Clarity:** To navigate a tumultuous world, above all else we use our awareness to cultivate clarity. This means being clear about when we have all the information and when we don't. It means knowing how fast to proceed in any direction. Do you need more information, or do you already know all you need for a clear yes or no?

- **Calling**: Yes or no should be easy, but it truly all depends on the attunement we have with our inner calling and deep understanding of our potential. Every decision we make is weighed against who we think we are and believe we are meant to become. Awareness is all about cultivating right standing with our identity and calling in alignment with our essence.

- **Confidence:** It is only once clarity is attained and is in perfect alignment with our calling that confidence becomes as natural as breathing. When confidence is not our natural state, something is not adding up. Not every step on this journey is going to be tread with absolute confidence, but just the awareness of when we are on track and when we are not is all the subtle and vital information we need to seek the council of our higher self.

Think of it this way: when real transformation occurs, it takes place at the level of identity. However, to change my perspective of who I am is not a trick or technique. It is not about embracing an alter-ego, but rather, giving myself full permission to cultivate a relationship with the one person I have always managed and used but have never really seen: myself.

On one level we truly do know ourselves. We know deeply the desires, dreams, and dreads that live in the dungeons of our minds. And yet, there is a whole universe of ourselves we are just uncovering. Our natural divinity. Our physical eyes look outward, while awareness opens the eyes within.

Plato encourages us to know ourselves. I can tell you: knowing ourselves requires us to trust ourselves as well.

The next three chapters will explore clarity, calling, and confidence, together creating the pillar of Awareness and the stability we need to continue on this journey.

IDENTITY / AWARENESS
Our Timeline in Everyday Eden

PAST	PRESENT	PRESENT
Natural	Multidimensional	Futurist
Masculine	Consciousness + Creation	Feminine
Conscious Left Brain	Balance + Alchemy	Unconscious Right Brain

(DIVINITY WHISPERS)

Wherever you find yourself,
you are here.
You are now.

If you question what to choose,
stop and listen
within
to the voice—

To the beat of your own heart.
Let this be life.
As you choose love.
As you choose peace.

As you choose the light that YOU ARE.

CHAPTER TWO
Clarity: Accessing the Crystalline Within

I had known him, whom I will call Nathan (meaning "gift of God"), since I was five years old. We grew up in a small but bustling mining town called Selebi-Phikwe in Botswana. It was my whole world. Between the "hakuna matata" attitude and the African wilderness, time felt endless growing up. We both went to the same primary school, and he was three years ahead. He was cute, and became a sports team captain. It is safe to say he was a big deal in my little eyes back then. A dream boat, you might say.

Nathan and I reconnected just shy of two months before my experience in the jungle and my awakening at the Mayan temple. I was doing my very first one-woman live show called Shine, based on my third internationally bestselling group book. I was so nervous and so excited about it, and it flowed so beautifully. I had incredible people helping me set it up, and the audience could not have loved it more. I knew what I wanted to do with my life. I wanted to teach. I wanted to sing. That's it. That's all I was born to do. It was natural to me. Teach and sing.

I was a whole new person. I was not here to be taken on a ride on any boat no matter how dreamy. Oh no, not I. I was twelve hours away from turning the ripe, wise age of forty-one and a freshly reborn Mayan priestess to boot. I had people to see, books to write, places to go. I had a fifteen-year corporate and executive career under my belt and was going on seven years as a freelance corporate trainer and executive coach. I was excited about world travel and leadership education. I was planning retreats in different parts of the world. It was so exhilarating, and the world was my oyster, as they say. So it felt. So it was.

And that's when I heard from him. A like on Facebook was about to alter the course of my humanity, and I didn't see it coming.

From the moment we got on the phone and I heard Nathan's voice, it was love. Everything from the volume to the accent to the tone and the laughter. He tickled me inside and out. It is bizarre when we do not gradually fall in love. It is different when it's just *there*, and there is no apparent reason. That was the truth from the first moment. We stayed on the phone for three hours that night, and pretty much every day that followed. When I was planning my trip to Mexico, I was going to be so close to him, and we decided to meet up.

Suddenly, there I was, in the luggage lounge at the Costa Rican airport trying to remember which bag was mine. Soon, I was standing outside, but didn't see him. People rushed toward me, asking if I wanted a taxi. I panicked a little and sent him a message: *I'm outside.* Nervous giggles bubbled to the surface.

Relief floods my system as he texted right back, *Just parking the car.* The moment I saw him ... Lord! My heart flew open. Oh, so dreamy. I knew this man. His embrace was warm, and I was instantly comfortable. He was more nervous, but then he saw that yes, I was indeed the same person. On and off the phone, or in person.

He had spoken to me for two months and didn't trust my word. He was nervous and chatty at first, making idle conversation but shaky in his actions. I could tell he was trying to make a good impression. I wondered, did he not remember how taken I already was with him? Did he not accept how much love I had already demonstrated by just being there with him, in his truck, homebound on the Costa Rican highway?

That was my first sign, and it totally blew over my head.

Into the truck we leapt, luggage secure, and then we were homebound to his little cabin in the jungle. We had spoken for hours. We had shared our hopes, our dreams, and our deepest desires. We had also shared our disappointments and our plans for the next steps. It was exactly 11:11 AM when we arrived at the gate, and I opened it, welcoming us home. The full moon hung heavy and vibrant in the sky as the eclipse in Leo performed its magnificent dance. I was home. I was whole. I was with him.

I sat on the cabin porch and took a deep breath. The morning was magnificent. The temperature was already twenty degrees Celsius, and a gentle breeze moved through the trees. The jungle in Costa Rica was different than in Mexico, even richer and more abundant with wildlife. Nathan came around the corner, a warm cup of coffee in hand and a goofy sweet smile on his face and handed it to me.

Our first night was everything I imagined and more. It was a completely new experience of effortless, gentle, natural, and loving connection. Like two pieces of a puzzle coming together.

"So, tell me again, what is it that you do exactly?" he asked. "I'd love to understand."

Multidimensional mastery is hard to explain in words. "Instead of trying to break it down, why don't I just show you," I said.

"Okay." He grinned, intrigued. He set his coffee down on the little wooden table and turned to me, open and curious. "What do I do?"

"Absolutely nothing." I smiled, tickled to share an experience I normally only share with my clients with him. "You only need to relax and to allow yourself to feel."

I started to guide him through the breath to relax. He surrendered and began to sense the field open as I sang. He could feel the love and the divine presence manifesting and the warmth of this energy. I then took him "up," as I call it. That is what it feels like even if we don't really go anywhere. The higher dimensions open and we simply become aware of them in present time and space. I asked him in this higher place to notice himself. "Where are you? What are you wearing? Is there anything you are doing?"

He perceived himself as a very tall, large, white warrior. He was dressed head to toe with armor made of some kind of steel or iron. He was standing with his back turned to a massive field of light. It felt comparable to a football field but many thousands of times larger. "It is a field of pure white light," he said, amazed. "I know that I am here to protect this. I am devoted to this light."

"Can you sense me in this place?"

"Yes. You are a queen in this place." He noticed me approach him, and he shuddered in reverence. He couldn't understand why I was approaching him, as there were thousands of warriors like him surrounding the field.

"I choose you, because I love you," I answered.

With that he began to take off his armor, piece by piece. I helped him remove the heavy, robust steel, and when he was free of all the weight of this protection, he could feel his celestial body. He felt amazing and looked at me again and whispered, "We are exactly the same." He asked if he could kiss me there and drew me to him. As we connected in the higher plains, I felt the orgasmic energy pass through my body. Every touch in the ethereal communicating in the physical. It was the most ecstatic and electrifying sexual energy I had ever experienced, while in everyday awareness, we were simply holding hands sitting on the cabin porch.

I smiled shyly, blushing, still recovering from the reflexive orgasm I was experiencing. We traveled in the other realm together and came to a place where he visited his mother, who had passed in 2008. He missed her, and she was his greatest love. He was emotional to see her and surprised at her cool and detached demeanor when, in just her style, she said, "Why are you missing me? Don't you know I could never leave you?" He knew this was true and allowed the peace of that to permeate his being. The love they shared could never be lost, and he remembered that now. After their embrace, we were ready to conclude our inter-dimensional travels. It was precious to feel this love and this tenderness, as well as the sexual and primal. This connection had activated energies and sensations I had never been aware of.

I brought him down again through the breath, and anchored him into the dimension we call the third dimension and everyday awareness. I will never forget the moment he looked at me. I had never felt more seen, more loved or treasured.

"How, do you do that?" He was in awe. "That was the most profound and real experience I've ever had. How is that even possible? And so easy and effortless."

Well, it was easy and effortless, and not at the same time. Not really. To truly flow, or fly as the case may be, it requires one vital and very important detail. It requires *unconditional trust to allow*. It needs us to be present and relaxed, open, and curious.

TWO PATHS TO CLARITY

This precious commodity, the ability to trust ourselves and be flexible enough to open to these new awarenesses, is the key to unlocking multidimensional mastery. This level of relaxation and openness is truly the only condition I have found to access our natural divinity and navigate through space and time with our higher self.

The masculine principle within requires us to know ourselves. You are not being told what is real; you simply allow yourself to experience, feel, and know for yourself. The feminine principle is the magic that recognizes and remembers the natural divine state, and that requires the second piece of the puzzle: to trust ourselves. Can we receive these messages, sensations, and experiences and actually believe and trust ourselves?

To know thyself is to know what is real. To trust thyself is coming to the end of the egoic construct of what you've believed is possible and to surrender to that which is divine, without fear. This is the way that the divine realms honor the universal and divine law of free will. The field, and all the guides that may share wisdom with us—like your higher self, the Ascended Masters, or an ancestor—will never tell you what is true, but the messages from them will always represent the highest level of information you need in the greatest expression of love, when you are ready to see it and hear it.

Clarity is the first step of awareness because without a clear knowing, we can't move forward in our empowerment.

It always amazed me how everyone seems so clear, like they know all the answers. From the time we are small children, we are told what is real, what is good, what is true, who is right. The minute I had a problem and shared it with the people in my life, they always seemed to have an answer. Inevitably, they had experienced a similar experience, and would proceed to tell me which steps to take. Except they didn't have the answers. Not really.

We can learn from everything and everyone, and indeed we do. But the truth is that every single moment is a unique perfect tone that has never existed before. This means that every single situation is different. How could anyone know the perfect, right thing for any other being? There is no clean cut right or wrong answer—to anything. So, this is where our mastery begins.

Can we learn to know and trust ourselves, so that we make decisions we can live with? In each moment, can we make the best choice we can with the information we have at the time? If we do anything because another told us to, without our inner conviction or peace, they will simply become someone we can blame and shame for our future discomfort or perceived misfortune. But as we talk about a path of empowerment, we truly need to own and be responsible for each step of our process.

As uncomfortable as this notion may feel, if we accept it only for a moment and take a breath, we start to see the absolute infinite wonderfulness and the challenge of the same idea.

Let me share an example of a pivotal decision from my life to illustrate this point. My dad, Tony Morais, was the person I trusted the most in my life. He was the person who provided for me and lead a very successful and honorable career as a sectional engineer in the mines of Botswana. He was a leader of many, and I knew that his love and care was my greatest council.

The day came when I knew in my bones it was time to leave my corporate career and start my own business. I had sat with guidance in prayer, I had received the signs and the confirmation, but when I announced my big decision to my family, my father's response was one of absolute disagreement and dismay.

"Start your own company, Lizete? What do you know about running a business?" he asked, glaring at me across the dinner table. His body was tense, and his frown communicated his deep discomfort and disbelief. My expression shifted suddenly from one of conviction and courage to cowering and scrambling for words. It was true that I knew nothing about business. Dad had also had a terrible experience starting his own business and becoming bankrupt. At all costs, he didn't want me to experience the same.

I understood and had compassion for all that. But starting my own business was the best career decision and boss move I have ever made, creatively, financially, and spiritually. It would only take three months for my dad to see the fruits that my decision was the right one, but only because I had the grit to do what I needed to do and what was right for me.

Only I know what is ultimately right for me, and I am the one who is going to live the consequence of my decisions. This is why we need to cultivate clarity in our own lives for our own selves. If we are wise, we will learn from others' mistakes, stories, and trajectories, but we need to know and trust ourselves as a unique creation. My dad didn't have my talents, gifts, or abilities, and I learned and am learning all I need to know about "business" along the way.

Recall a time you were in a situation and couldn't see a way out. Your back was against the wall, and you had to make a decision. Right or left—something had to shift. Perhaps you shared your dilemma with someone, and they told you about the time they faced a similar challenge. They shared their insights, recommendations, advice and, if you were really lucky, the resources to head in the same direction.

Sometimes moments like these feel like heaven. Like home. For me, there were moments when I just wept with relief as the answer to a prayer was given and I saw the way clearly lit like the rising of a new dawn after a long night of doubt and darkness. I felt my life force return and a certainty in my steps moving forward. These are moments of clarity.

But there are also times when the guidance or the "normal thing people do" just will not work. We can't figure it out, but there is just something not right with it. This intuition can be a slight whisper and a gentle touch of discomfort or can feel like everything screaming at us from every cell of our bodies. But that's the path that worked for everyone else, right? So, we take it anyway.

As the circumstances of our choices unfold, we call it many names. Bad luck. Karma. Injustice. Assholes. Bad advice. The state of humanity. Demonic spiritual warfare. We project and blame the circumstances, feeling that we had no other choice. That was me until I understood what clarity is truly all about.

Both of these situations—where things feel perfect and work out and when they feel terrible and don't work out—are examples of clarity. One is just a longer and more painful way to get there. When we don't make choices based on alignment with our intuitive intelligence and higher consciousness, we have to work it out in life through challenging situations until we will learn the lesson.

This is the reason that clarity is our first step in this journey of freedom, empowerment, and embodiment of our natural divinity. If we are to be sovereign, whole beings, then we need to be free to choose. Our freedom of choice is the most precious thing. But we cannot choose if we are not connected with our inner clarity. This is especially true when we are so sure of our ways and overly eager to outsource our power to another to fix it.

Wherever you are right now in your life as you read these words, this will always be true: *You are infinite potential. You are deeply loved. You have the key within you. The only thing you will need to let go of is the idea that you have it all figured out.*

CLAIMING YOUR MULTIDIMENSIONALITY

Clarity is the level of light we are navigating in and literally using to create our reality. On this journey of wholeness, we learn to master clarity by healing our fear of the dark. We learn to see in the dark. We learn to open our spiritual and ancient inner knowing of the cosmic heart, and we start creating what I call crystalline clarity.

Ultimately, crystalline clarity is congruence within all five levels of your being: mental, emotional, physical, etheric, and soul/divine consciousness. As conscious creators, we are always creating. This means we get to choose how to spend our life force in each moment.

What I discovered was that the more I raised my level of light—my frequency, in other words—the more I was able to make choices that led to greater and greater freedom. You may have heard many spiritual guides or mystics talk about raising frequency, and I hope that this understanding of clarity gives you a new understanding. Raising frequency is nothing more than willing that the lights be turned on higher. It is fueled by the desire to know what is true, good, and real instead of the story that has served as a comfortable illusion. Higher frequency, more light, and crystalline clarity afford us more authentic connection with ourselves. This journey does have its cost, but it the path that leads to what some call magic, miracles, and synchronicities. Everything begins working out. Every project succeeds, every wish manifests. Some in ways we could not have imagined.

The most empowering revelation I can share with you is that you are a multidimensional being. What that means is that you exist in multiple dimensions all at once, and that you can access all wisdom across time and space. It sounds like a lot, I know! So, let's break it down. We can have access to the light and we can cultivate the light within us—but how do we co-create and actually use the light, that brings up the truth and matters that require our attention, and begin to manifest better outcomes and more harmonious solutions?

First, we start with nature. There are five main elements, a concept that is found in many philosophical, religious, and spiritual traditions. They are known to be the main building blocks of all of life:

- **Air:** The invisible and most important first element for all life on Earth. Without air, we would stop living within moments. Genesis 2:7 states: "And the Lord God formed man of the dust of the ground and breathed into his nostrils the breath of life; and man became a living being." I believe this is the element of air. When we take in the life, intention, understanding, and mind of our natural divine intelligence, we become a living sovereign being.

- **Water:** We have always heard that water is *the* sign that life anywhere is possible, and so we understand the without water there is no life. We are made up of 70 to 80 percent water and this is where our crystalline DNA is stored. The waters within us are the waters we want to stir, purify, and regenerate. While the universe is mind and starts with the air, it is infused in the waters to bring about life.

- **Earth:** The third dimension and physical plane of matter, where we see the manifest result of air and water into physical, carbon-based matter. The form may be a gigantic mountain range or a tiny little frog. Regardless of what it is, the planetary consciousness of the Earth has created form from it an initial concept and design. Earth is our third element and divinity manifest. This was the beauty I understood in the jungle. The divine was not something far away in the sky that I had to appease, but rather the incredibly real, practical, and beautiful manifest creation we are already a part of.

- **Fire:** The element of fire has come to mean the power of change and transformation. We often state that the only constant in life is change, but what is creating the change? Why can't it stay the same? I believe the reason is that fire is the natural and supernatural element that causes all movement and all of nature to evolve, transform, and come into a different and new form. Fire is the element that creates alchemy.

- **Space/Ether:** The final frontier indeed, and the last of the elements, Space is the place that allows for the material to manifest and prove itself. It is space and time in the moment of now that we can see what things truly are. We see the result of all the decisions, choices, and the inner workings that are now perceivable in form as the result or effect of the cause we have chosen.

Next, within ourselves there are five bodies, a concept that describes the layers of our being. While often I hear about these five as aspects or "levels" of our being, I like to call them "bodies." They each function and operate in their own way—and yet, just like the elements, each has their own unique way of sharing information with the others to create a unified whole. We often mistakenly see ourselves as one solid block of matter, but once we realize that we have five specific bodies with different needs and architecture, nurturing ourselves becomes a new art form, allowing various things to be true at the same time.

Here are the five bodies:

- **Mental:** Our mind is the most powerful processing machine within creation. We take in millions of bits of information at any moment, and every single second of our existence is recorded within the vast halls of our unconscious and subconscious mind. Our mental body likes to create order from chaos, so based on our culture, upbringing, beliefs, and needs we create boxes to store, file, and archive our thoughts. Thoughts become things we have often heard. We actively perpetuate circumstances by our perception and how we understand the opportunities around us. The mental body is not who we are but rather the operating console from where we navigate and make our choices.

- **Emotional:** The waters of our being and how we feel about things is truly what moves us. All motion comes from the emotion we are feeling based on our thoughts, past experiences, stories, and beliefs about our circumstances. The emotional body is immense, very much like the ocean, with its ebb and flow and constant motion. It cannot be confined or manipulated, and does not operate within time or space. There are emotions we can try to repress and push down, however just like a ball we try to keep down in the swimming pool, the longer we hold and deeper we hold it down, the quicker and more explosively it rushes to the surface.

- **Physical:** Our physical body, which is what we most commonly think of as a body, still requires a complete reintroduction. It was only upon the completion of my three-month Essential Ecosystem experience that I met and connected with my physical body in a whole new way. It is unfathomable how much misinformation we have about ourselves. From our earliest years, we absorb and accept lies regarding aging, disease, and weight gain, and through this acceptance we perpetuate a cycle of suffering generation upon generation. Within my work, I have found the body to be incredibly adaptable and able to regenerate and heal itself if given the correct, safe, and nurturing environment. Our body literally responds to our ecosystem and environment. It is an intelligent and eternally faithful living temple to house our inner being and manifest on the outside what is or has happened on the inside.

- **Energetic:** Our physical, emotional, mental bodies are all contained within our energetic field or aura, which is also our astral body. This is how we move through time and space with the fire that creates our circumstances and changes our situations. It is the most mystical of bodies and responds to the frequency and vibration of our life. This has been passed down through our ancestral line and is directly connected to where we choose to operate from energetically. The frequency of love, peace, and joy creates a more harmonious field which is the energetic body. This is liberating when you realize that you truly are in control of what is in your field and what is not. We then use the fire element to alchemize what is out of alignment with the new creation in the present moment.

- **Multidimensional:** Our soul body or multidimensional body is beyond even the field of the present moment and this present understanding of existence, and can be seen partly as the higher self. This is the space holder of our ultimate potential—our soul body and the one who knows us as infinite. This is where wisdom is nurtured and is the container that holds the space for our becoming. As we work with the other elements (all of which fill this space), we notice the results and feedback of life as the multidimensional body. This is where we see the result of harmonization of each of the individual elements coming into one as a single manifestation.

Finally, there are five main dimensions that we are interested in. There are many more than five dimensions; I personally know and have experienced up and including the thirteenth dimension. For the purposes of this book, however, we will focus on the first five.

These five dimensions are intrinsically connected to the five elements and the five bodies. I like to understand them as follows:

- **First Dimension:** Everything that is alive today started in some form as a seed, us included. Each of us was born from a seed of a man, and that seed is the divine spark we each are. We came with unique gifts, talents, and abilities that make us an individual.

- **Second Dimension:** The mother's womb is the second dimension. Within these waters, we found safety, comfort, and a place to grow. The intelligence encoded in the seed itself knew how to grow all of our fingers, toes, organs, and hair. There was nothing that anyone had to do to teach us how to grow and evolve from a seed into a human; it is the intelligence each of us carries. It is the intelligence of our nature.

- **Third Dimension:** The dimension of form is when we are born in a human body to our family. We are given a name and an identity, and we quickly forget the safety, warmth, and provision of our mother's womb. Each of us have different responsibilities and rules that we accept and follow to belong to the family unit or society we are born into. This dimension of reality seems very fixed and permanent, yet it is everything but. Every moment of every day, we are growing and changing, the outside forces now informing and having their consequences. There is nothing about any person that is stuck in time if we no longer want it to be, and yet there are clear needs and guidelines for anybody to have a healthy, vital, and strong physical form.

- **Fourth Dimension:** The easiest way to explain the fourth dimension is as the transformational or transmutational unseen energetic force that is facilitating our becoming through time and space. As we discern and change our ideas and feelings about certain subjects, the physical vessel is held and supported by the energetic field. As Jeshua said, we will reap what we sow, and He was indeed explaining the quantum field in ways that could be easily understood.

- **Fifth Dimension:** The fifth dimension is the cosmic portal to our higher self and is the connection between our eternal self, the soul that has always been with the divine and now operates as a fractal of itself in the here and now, as an individual vessel. This is the part of you that is eternal and has access to all higher dimensions. Once we have entered the fifth dimension, we have entered into a state of unity and wholeness, embodying and integrating all dimensions.

Now that you have an understanding of each of these separately, the elements, bodies, and dimensions can be paired together to create a comprehensible framework, which is how we'll be navigating the rest of this book:

- **Air/Mental Body/First Dimension:** This is where all thought, imagination, memory, and moments of time have been infinitely imprinted. Divided into the conscious, subconscious, and unconscious minds, this is our *intellectual intelligence* and the greatest processing creation on planet Earth.

- **Water/Emotional Body/Second Dimension**: This is where all timeless DNA wisdom and knowledge is held and crystallized. The ancestral genes communicate and form the emotional impulses and information that speaks to our waters. This is also where programmed and primordial (preexistent) information is stored. This is our *intuitive intelligence*—the place where truth is known, felt, and remembered.

- **Earth/Physical Body/Third Dimension**: This is the plane where all our thoughts and memories become a manifest physical body or circumstance. It is the result of our divine co-creation with the ancestral line of humanity—our collective experience, and our personal experience right here in our bodies. This is our *innate intelligence*, the one who knows the ways of the divine and is the apex of all creation.

- **Fire/Energetic Body/Fourth Dimension:** This is the plane of our evolution. The area or aura we call the individual forcefield or torus informs our entire being within the quantum field in which we are held. This is our hidden and obscured, and most urgently needed, inner power to transmute or transform any and every circumstance. Our access to our divinity. Our divine love! This is our *sentinel intelligence*.

- **Space/The Multidimensional Master/Fifth Dimension:** This is the space you and I occupy on this planet and the contribution we make to our loved ones. The result and fruit of that investment is the reality we co-create. We are writing the script to the experience which will be known as our human lives right here and now. This is the *sovereign and instinctual intelligence*.

This framework is not a magic pill or secret family recipe; it is simply a roadmap for the journey we are navigating. The beginning of clarity is to know that all intelligence, all solutions, and all creative innovation is already inside you. I hope your use of this will bring understanding and empowerment for you to effectively change the circumstances around you and create the life you feel in your waters.

IDENTITY / CLARITY
Navigating within the Matrix

AIR ELEMENT

Mental Body
Thoughts
First Dimension

WATER ELEMENT

Emotional Body
Feelings
Second Dimension

FIRE ELEMENT

Energetic Body
Creation + Sexuality
Fourth Dimension

EARTH ELEMENT

Physical Body
Manifestation
Third Dimension

Each sacred soul of humanity has been born with a purpose and a pulse for something unique and extraordinary. Why this information is so important is only so we can understand, or have a framework to work from, that supports the understanding that we truly do have it all within us. We have not been taught to effectively care, nurture, and support ourselves to grow naturally, or at least this was my case.

Overweight, overworked, and depleted for over two decades from my early twenties until my forty-fourth birthday, I never dreamed how much I could transform. Until I learned these secrets. Until I understood that everything is indeed energy, and only by mastering my internal energy would the external adjust and be transmuted into greater peace, greater safety, and more alignment. As it did, my body responded. These explanations don't give you how to navigate this incredible understanding of the new divine blueprint, which is our natural birthright, but that is why we have a full twelve-step process. We will be building on this understanding and dissecting the needs, insights, and information to support the whole journey throughout the rest of the book. This understanding is the foundation of co-creating our reality with our higher self.

It is a comforting and revolutionary thought that we arrived with everything we need, and we leave with everything we choose to do with our time, gifts, talents, and essence. This is so different to the current paradigm where we come with nothing and leave with nothing. I believe this is a pivotal point for humanity. We truly do have it all within us. Just like Nathan and I did sitting on that porch together, his hand in mine, traveling the universe together and experiencing our beautiful light bodies. The happiest and most joyful place in all my world. Making peace with all of darkness. Unfortunately, the rest of our love story would not unfold quite the same way—but we'll get to that soon.

The transmutation and transformation of this deep-seated truth in its perfect wholeness has become the core of the creation of ARISE, the activation of my most sovereign realization and the uncovering of my sacred spiritual gifts.

That did not take place in one meditation. It has been a journey with life to understand its benevolence—an evolutionary process of learning how not to resist life but to understand that healing our wounds is necessary, and we have all been wounded.

This process has cycles and iterations that we learn to hold space for and be with in compassion as much as we can. The goal is connecting with our higher selves and cosmic consciousness while holding safe nurturing and loving space for the whole of us and others. Natural divinity emerges through the crystalline clear vibration of loving surrender and trust that life is for us. Now, we learn to walk with life and access our creative energies and powers in an evolutionary process.

CHAPTER THREE
Calling: The Attitude of Purpose

I have always been a seeker. Why am I here? What am I here to do? What will I be and experience? I am constantly looking to answer these questions. But one answer I never expected was what my friend told me one day.

"You were born to lead a revolution!"

The blood drained out of my face, and I felt my heart sink, a deep sorrow invading me. So many dreams I still wanted to fulfill. So many wonderful moments I longed to feel and live and share, with so many people I haven't even had the deepest honor to meet yet. I had retreats to run, things to share, ceremonies to experience.

I personally had always wanted to experience the face of God. I longed to experience what that glory could be like. And in an intimate moment beside a tree at six years old, I remember bowing my head and just whispering to Spirit under my breath, "Just show me who I need to be."

That's what I'd always wanted, and yet, in a moment when I was being told clearly who I needed to be, my immediate response was to shrink away in fear. Revolution! Shit. That was the only thing that I had zero—and I mean zero—time for.

My beautiful, patient friend sat and silently witnessed my longing for a life not yet lived. She understood. She too had seen the dark. She, too, had sat in the cave, just waiting to come alive. She gently rocked me in the space of her silence. I felt her love. And what she did next forever changed my life.

She said, "Beloved. Maybe you have not understood what revolution means."

Silence.

Maybe I had not. What did she know that I didn't? I leaned in and listened. Really listened. It was the moment she said the magical words that set me free to the level of consciousness I can now share this work with you.

"Revolution means the evolution revealed."

A waterfall of relief flooded my system. Revolution had nothing to do with ending a war, except for the one inside myself. Instead, it was about peace. The power of peace, expressed through you and I as human beings.

THE CLAIMING OF OUR CALLING

We began with clarity, which helps us to understand what is real, who is who, what is where. Our immediate next question becomes, "Okay, then why?" This is the next step in our Essential Ecosystem: calling.

"What is my purpose?" is the most frequently asked question in my coaching and mentoring practice. We all have a deep longing to know what we are meant to do, why we are here. This is our calling. Knowing our purpose answers the Big Why of our soul. Knowing it and connecting with it keeps us motivated because, even though we might not be where we long to be, if we know we are on the right path, we are willing to keep going. Knowing we are on track connects us to power, harmony, and balance. The very point of each of us—all distinct, unique individuals—is to have our own natural divine experience. To create our own legacy—our own life story.

Understanding our calling is powerful because it subconsciously and unconsciously informs and directs almost every single decision we make. As we navigate our every day, we only have our yes and no. When we are clear about our calling, we can more confidently make decisions that will lead us toward it.

One of the most pivotal revelations that informs this understanding is the idea that perspective and attitude are everything. When we connect with our calling, we are activating the highest clarity, sitting at the highest vantage point—a great place to see everything and make our decisions from. It also means we are allowing ourselves to be open and nonjudgmental about what might come through. Cultivating an ability to listen to our higher self in everyday reality is a key part of this process. Sometimes things might not have immediate outcomes, but there are so many exciting adventures when we have our eye on the prize.

We truly are the adventure, dear one. Within the ARISE Academy we have a saying: You are the secret! We are the secret being revealed to us. Within a meditation one day, I was asking Jeshua about the upcoming plans to write this book and the launch of the ARISE Academy. As I had been walking with Him for a very long time already, I asked Him, "How will this cycle be different? What is the one thing I need to avoid to prevent self-sacrifice or self-sabotage?"

I knew I was following my calling, but I was also hoping to avoid failing again. Although our experiences are never failures, when we build only to lose over and over again, we are more hesitant to try. I wanted to learn from my "mistakes" to avoid repeating them. His answer stunned me into silence as He revealed that core reason why previous episodes had not delivered the rewards, fruits, or promises I had hoped for.

He gently said, "What ruins things is your need to be someone."

My need to *be* someone? Am I not someone already? Well, of course I am someone; however, the someone I knew myself to be did not always think that I was enough to truly accomplish my goals. In other words, the biggest fear programming that any individual will ever have to transmute is the sneaky little voice that questions if we are enough. This has been layered on through eons of time with societal, familial, and cultural programming. The simple message is that we are not enough as we are. That we are small, insignificant, and fragile. We are often questioned and tested—are we intelligent enough or beautiful enough? In our survival programming, these are the two triggers that get pushed most often, and if we have any self-doubt, the manipulation to take us out of our center simply works.

The lesson I got from this conversation with Jeshua was the calibration that no matter what I produce or create, the only value I can truly offer is who I really am. My calling is to have peace and acceptance with that. No one else can do it for me, and nothing anyone says can remove the sting of self-rejection.

Our calling can only be to be ourselves, dear one, because that is truly the only thing we have. That we truly can be. Finding the value, beauty, expression, and gift of this being is the invitation of our multidimensional mastery. As we learn to know and trust ourselves, we also learn to accept that we can only give what we authentically are. No more and no less. Our healing work is to heal all the spaces where the idea that we were not enough has hurt us, betrayed us, and caused us to abandon ourselves.

So, how do we do this? How do we stay true to ourselves, using the lens of energy? This is the alchemy we are learning about within these pages.

CLAIMING OUR MULTIDIMENSIONALITY

Let us dive deeper into our multidimensionality and see what we have to work with. It's glorious, I promise. Through the incredible work of the honorable late scientist David Hawkins, we are given seventeen states of consciousness.

A fundamental principle to understanding this idea is that everything is energy, including ourselves, trees, animals, clothing, companies—everything! Some music immediately puts you in a good space—that's energy. You can sense when your friend or partner is in a bad mood—that's energy. Each energy has a different frequency associated with it, which refers to the shape and power of that energy. We variously experience these states of consciousness, but all of them are available and present for us at all times.

Dr. Hawkins created his trademarked Map of Consciousness as a way to systematically measure the energy of different states of being. The Map outlines the seventeen states of consciousness and assigns them logarithmic numbers. This allowed him to define where any person, place, or thing fell on the scale of consciousness. For our purposes, we will just focus on the states themselves, which from highest frequency to lowest are: Enlightenment, Peace, Joy, Love, Reason, Acceptance, Willingness, Neutrality, Courage, Pride, Anger, Desire, Fear, Grief, Apathy, Guilt, and Shame.

The purpose of this categorization is understanding that your personal energetic calibration is representative of your context for experiencing everything. These are the choices we have available to us at any moment. It is this context that creates meaning around what we experience. When we understand these frequencies, we understand what we are creating in each moment with our yes and our no. Are we basing ourselves in pride, or in love and joy? Deciding this consciously is embodying consciousness. Not more and not less. Peace has been my free will choice for a long time because it is the one state that takes me to the next natural state—enlightenment.

This variation in frequency is why two people can experience the same thing but have completely different reactions to it. When we are each operating in our own individual frequency, the intention of where we are coming from will either create harmony or chaos. Neither one is higher nor better than the other. We need things to break apart when they don't work, and we need to put things together and harmonize them in order for them to develop. Both are growth and both are a choice. This is the sacred responsibility of each of them. We each have these seventeen frequencies within us.

As Proverbs 23:7 says: "For as a man thinks within himself, so he is. 'Eat and drink!' he'll say to you, but his heart won't be with you." How we make choices moment by moment is determined first and most notably by how we perceive ourselves, who we understand ourselves to be on an identity level. What are our options? What do we believe we are allowed to do? Allowed to *be*? We have it all within our imagination, but we have to be able to release our expectations and societal conditioning. This is the dance we are sorting and what is co-creating our external reality and circumstances.

So how do you want to experience the world? When looking at those states, the obvious choices are the higher frequencies. But to harness this true power of choice, we come back to the fact that we are multidimensional beings. Some of these choices are happening on a conscious level while others are all activating on a subconscious and unconscious level.

After my experience at the Mayan temple in Mexico, I started to think about how to integrate these frequencies and states of consciousness into my understanding of the elements and the bodies that make up our anatomy, as introduced in the previous chapters. In order to build a life, we need to choose wisely who is building that life with us. Our Essential Ecosystem is always focused on how we are personally navigating our life, yet the people we choose to trust are the ones who co-create and inhabit the environment we have manifested.

I lay under the covers, the duvet heavy around me as I welcomed its comfort. I felt as if I had been crying for days without relief. I didn't have the energy. Mom softly came to the door, opening it just enough.

"You okay, love?"

Silence would answer that question more eloquently than any word I could conjure surely. I simply stirred, clearing my throat. She ventured in gently and sat on the bed. She looked at me as I returned her blue piercing gaze. There was no worry. There was no haste. There was no concern. Only deep understanding and love. A deep knowing I would be okay. My mother is a mighty fortress, and I had never seen it until I was broken in a million pieces, laying in that bed, looking up at her.

I told her, through a mouth dry from weeping, "I can't find the end of it."

"The end of what, love?" She leaned in.

"The end of my love, Mom. I'm trying to find the end of this vastness so I can finally be over it. I cannot find the end. I still love him."

I had returned to Mom's house after a horrible fight with Nathan. We'd spent two and a half years building our home, and I'd just walked away with two hundred euros and bags of broken promises and dreams.

Cycles of gaslighting, mood swings, healing, and then harmony. For a little while, at least, the moments of heaven kept me raptured. Walking away from everything I had dreamed was the hardest thing I have ever done in my life. Leaving cost me literally everything except the clothes on my back and my last grain of sanity.

Now, Mom received me home now in Sao Martinho do Porto, Portugal, a historical fishing town that has always showed up in my life when I most needed a change in direction.

I am so grateful that I spent a lifetime on my spiritual development and personal development to meet myself here. In that moment of despair, I reached out to the divine. That is truly the only place to go in these moments of death. When life seemed to fall apart, I awaited guidance. Spirit met with me in that place and when the whisper came, I was surprised.

Are you willing to forgive?

I felt in deeper. Did I hear that right? The question came again.

Are you willing to forgive?

Could I forgive? I was in the deepest pain I had ever experienced. This was worse than death because it was chosen. It was inflicted. Could I forgive?

Well, yes. Yes, I absolutely could. And I will tell you why.

I knew this man who had broken my heart. His family, his home, and his accent. I understood his boarding school trauma and I loved his stories. I heard of the wars he had literally fought during his twenty-three year career as a military man. I witnessed the genius those same years had equipped him with, growing every skill he needed to engineer and build our home from thought alone.

I understood it all. I saw the dire dysfunction and deeply felt the devastating desire. Yes. Of course, I could forgive. Nathan and I had talked about this during one of our endless and infinite romantic nights of sharing, with our favorite playlist softly humming against the backdrop of the Costa Rican jungle. We loved cooking together and talking when the mood allowed. Sitting in our rocking chairs, we talked about seeing things from the other's perspective.

We need devotional love to actually listen to each other, because once we understand, forgiveness is possible. Until that point, we hold to our judgment of what is different.

The pursuit of developing our multidimensional mastery is not different. The main skill we are developing is something I had read in the sacred scriptures a million times and never quite understood. The power to have the eyes to see and the ears to hear. Will we listen, will we choose to understand. Do we choose to forgive?

The yes permeated my being. Love released and moved, filling my field. The agony of my loss had me paralyzed, but the free will choice of forgiveness liberated that energy within my body. This was an initiation into understanding the power of regeneration and the power of choice we have as we unlock our fire.

Let us come back to our beautiful seventeen frequencies to choose from and the understanding that we are always making a single yes or no choice. I looked at these frequencies many times until I could see that there was one that was the game changer: fear. The divine frequency will never go below fear because it is in violation of free will. It would override the sovereignty of humankind. It is our choice to fear that justice will not prevail. Instead, we can choose love and focus on the higher frequencies.

This single choice—forgiveness—was not about condoning, agreeing with, or repeating past behavior. It was about taking my power back. It was about retrieving my innate divinity to alchemize the damage done. The one single choice in Christ Consciousness we develop within ARISE is choosing love over fear.

That is why we focus next on confidence.

Before we get there though, let's look at the sixteen frequencies and how they fit perfectly in with the four dimensions and bodies.

- **Air/Mental Body:** Enlightenment, Peace, Joy, and Love. These are the primary foundational frequencies of Christed Consciousness and where all mental health and well-being begin. These are also the divine masculine qualities.

- **Water/Emotional Body:** Reason, Acceptance, Willingness, and Neutrality. These are the divine attributes of the feminine side. While water can be destructive—think of floods or tsunamis—we prefer our internal waters to be calm and serene. By choosing these states of being we are also calming our nervous system and boosting our immune system.

- **Earth/Physical Body:** Courage, Pride, Anger, and Desire. These four states speak to the impulses that drive us as human beings. We move forward in courage. Our motivation for our life choices is for others to be proud of us and for self-pride. Doing what we believe is the best for us and others is the most intimate and personal drive for every person. Anger and desire are the last two frequencies and serve as the main alchemy I have found within my research.

- **Fire/Energetic Body:** Grief, Apathy, Guilt, and Shame. These frequencies have been demonized for centuries, but they are our hidden treasure trove. Our humanity can be purified when the flame that burns is one of love and rebirth. Indeed, this very process we are talking about. I had to transform my desire into passion instead of anger by facing the grief, apathy, guilt, and shame I carried in my own field. I spent all my time, effort, and love on "fixing" the other—but I forgot that only Spirit can do that—and only *if we are willing*.

IDENTITY / CALLING
The Multidimensional Human

AIR ELEMENT

Mental Body
Masculine
Enlightenment
Peace, Joy, Love

WATER ELEMENT

Emotional Body
Feminine
Reason, Acceptance
Willingness, Neutrality

FIRE ELEMENT

Energetic Body
Masculine
Freedom
Grief, Apathy, Guilt, Shame

EARTH ELEMENT

Physical Body
Feminine
Loved and Loving
Courage, Pride, Anger, Desire

These four elemental states sum up all of the mainstream motivations and meta programs we see on the world stage. They are also the inner incentives of every human being and a common dream among us all. There are a few shifts I will discuss later in the book, but this is our solid foundation. The heart wants what the heart wants; this is our desire. However, we need to alchemize anger into passion for the driving force to be productive instead of destructive. If there is still anger around our desires, there is still some work to do.

When I chose forgiveness, I was activating my fire. I could use my fire to blast Nathan. Talk to his family, take revenge. But this is only a form of self-destruction. Or I could choose to forgive, letting the fire alchemize the lead into gold, returning the love to myself.

This was my quest. This was my calling: to transform and transmute all the grief and shame I had been given and return it to love within myself. For me. For my family. For my ancestral tree. For the world. For all of us. Each of us impacts our world. Each one of our energies matters, and as we awaken to this reality, caring for other becomes synonymous with caring for self. We begin to end separation. This is our power and inherent opportunity.

When we choose this, we are given something more precious than gold. We are given words that create our new world. Words that create a new reality where we are seen, received, loved, and cherished. When we choose ourselves first, gifts we never knew we had are activated.

It felt counterintuitive to share the story of the deepest pain of loss I have ever felt as the story for this chapter of calling. Even for me. Most teachers would talk about how to strengthen yourself, show up in your gifts, and step up into calling. This is not wrong, but here I shared with you the side that has been forgotten. It was so confusing to navigate, yet it has become the greatest portal of my natural divinity.

Chapter Three — Calling: The Attitude of Purpose

When my relationship with Nathan blew up on that terrible day in 2021, my faith, hope, and trust in humanity was shattered in a million pieces. It meant the loss of the person I most loved in the world and the home I built side-by-side with my beloved for two and a half years. It was the destruction of my dream and the place I believed I was bringing the leaders I would teach, support, and activate in the future. When I lost Nathan, I lost myself—or so I thought.

That dark night of the soul, that blanket of night, opened my heart and the light broke through. In the search for calling, many of us—perhaps even you, dear reader—have suffered loss. I offer this story for the simple reason that I want to share with you the deepest and most important lesson on calling. Your calling is not about anyone else. It is about *you*. It is about you accepting that which did not choose you, that which was lost, and that which is not present. This is the way you come to know that what you are, where you are, and who you are is more than enough at all times.

Our calling then becomes an exciting journey into consciousness and creation where we can just be with self and cultivate that self to express the gifts within. Many times, those gifts are so natural to you, so easy and graceful, that you think they are normal. But your love is not normal. It is supernatural. You have to learn to value and honor them as I did, especially in the face of those who gaslit or insulted you, ignorant of the beauty and value you bring.

I did die that day, no doubt. I was buried alive. It was an ego death—my ego was deconstructed and laid to rest. I had come to the end of that version of myself. I put myself in the Earth metaphorically, living a life I didn't want, caught in a nightmare totally out of my control. If you are experiencing that kind of moment, know that you still have everything inside of you for your calling.

When I lay on the ground, broken, I still had a choice.

My choice was, and is, to ARISE. This is my calling, and if you choose it, beloved, it can be yours, too.

We have covered the different frequencies that describe us all—what is within us to work with as we each find our unique path and complete our individual healing journey. I could not heal Nathan as he was not willing to receive healing. I had to learn that the only healing I needed to do was within myself.

Today I serve as a mere example. An imperfect, sensitive student of the mystery that we are unraveling and exploring together. The healing that is truly required is not the healing of a broken body, for the body will heal given the right ecosystem. Rather, it is the healing of the confidence to know that, in spite of every manifestation that has assured us that we are not special, we can have faith and find the inner wisdom that we are always more than enough.

(A CALL TO RETURN HOME)

We have waited lifetimes to be here.
We've prepared and learned and grown,
to be ready.
How much love can we be?
How much light can we activate?
The darkest night brings forth
the brightest of light
to create form.

The suffering we feel
is the imbalance.
This was not the plan, nor the design.
The design is perfect.
Do you not have eyes to see?

Then have ears to hear.
The design is perfect.
You and I are the design, beautiful one,
who is so loved, so loved,
so loved by the whole universe.

*Receive the love that you are
and your suffering will ease.
Cry the love you feel
and the light will come.
Be good to those around you
and your heart will heal.*

*How much love can you be?
That is all we need to do.
We must remember now
that we are love.
That what we care about
is love—and this is not for the spiritual,
or the scientific, or for the agnostic or the Christian or
the Jew, or all the little boxes
we've created for ourselves.
It is for humanity.*

*The ones of a human soul.
The ones of the spark of love.
The ones of the truth, and the light,
and the Mother.
Gaia wants only these ones.
And the world will shake
until only what's left
is what is built on the consciousness of Christ.
So, that is our work.
That is our work*

(A Call to Return Home)

*Us, embodying the consciousness that was modeled by
our brother, the love of God, the love of each other,
and the truth of the quantum.
That miracles are our birthright.
The activation of our light body
our joy, our bliss,
the truth of frequency and vibration and free will—
none of it contradicts.
Open your mind.
You are bigger than what you think you are.
And you are so loved.*

*But do not wait. Heal your heart.
Strengthen your empowerment, your
independence, your sustainability
and self-sufficiency. Wait for no one.
Do it for yourself, and it will be for everyone else.
We are waiting for you. You are waiting for us.
We and you, and you and I,
and I and we, and we are all of us.
We are you.
You are us.
There is no one
to channel anymore.
When the soul remembers it is god consciousness embodied,
you are the highest authority on the face of the Earth.*

You are free by your very existence beloved,
and yet you are not above another being.
Do you understand this?
Honor life and choose love.
Be whole again.
Do what it takes to recover every piece of
your soul that has been left behind,
And come home.

CHAPTER FOUR
Confidence: The Natural Power of You

Confidence should be our natural state, and indeed it is what we are healing within the pillar of awareness. When we are naturally feeling confident, it is because we are taking this next step with clarity in the sure direction of our calling; there is an alignment to free will and divinity. When confidence needs to be hard won, when we need to convince another of something or there is trembling in our step, we may need to look again.

After my fight with Nathan and my return to my mother's home, days turned into weeks, and weeks into months. It had been about nine months of back and forth. The highest insights, the deepest downloads from Spirit and Jeshua and then the darkest moments of death. I began working with the divine in closer harmony and synchronicity, and received so many clear instructions. Spirit shared that I was to teach on natural divinity, that I would hold retreats and gatherings. I was to sing the classic songs of the icons and new songs not yet heard. This was magical and I longed for that future, but then there were weeks when there was only weeping, grieving, and missing a life and love lost. Nathan and I would speak every day for fifteen minutes, thirty minutes, or one hour, but there was no solace or soul in it. He said he didn't want to let me go. I didn't want to let him go either.

I started to understand I was channeling a body of work. It was nothing I had been taught; instead, I was remembering it from another time and space. I was to find a new strategy, a new service, and an integrated way of sharing myself with the world again. It was to be a podcast, called the Wholeness Wisdom Well, a name that Spirit shared with me. I let out a yelp of excitement. I was ready and so excited. This solitude had been brutal, and I wanted to move forward again.

Instead, Spirit did something very unexpected. I clearly heard, *Fast and pray for seven days and seven nights. We will create a whole new world.*

I didn't know what to make of it. I asked, "Where do I go?" Immediately, two guy friends I'd previously had relationships with came to mind. Both relationships ended for very different reasons and at different times in my life, and I was surprised that this was Spirit's suggestion. No matter—I knew that Spirit would provide. I sent them both a text.

"Hey! Hope you're well. I'm looking for a small place out in nature that I could spend seven days to fast and pray. If you have any ideas, please let me know." I don't think I had ever been that clear in communicating my needs to them and I giggled as I put away my phone and drank my morning coffee. To my surprise, barely five minutes passed before I had a reply.

Mr. T offered a perfect little cabin in the woods where I would be alone. Mr. E could connect me with a community he knew through some landscaping work, and they had some cabins and yurts for rent. My feeling chose instantly. I called the community called Enxara, situated near Lisbon, Portugal, and spoke to the owner, Arthur. After a brief introduction, I explained I was looking for a quiet place in nature to retreat. The community had very low fees of twenty euros a night, and it came with three meals a day. It sounded like absolute heaven.

That was the first time I noticed Spirit speaking to me in real time. Or at least, I was finally listening. Within twenty-four hours I had packed a few things for the week, groomed my little dog, a Lhasa Apso named Sami, and we were off.

I drove up the driveway as the big gate was opened. A large farmhouse stood prominently, surrounded by gently swaying trees. I also saw various other buildings and a dome as I parked the car, trying to figure out where the reception was.

A quirky, squinting lady stepped out of the house with an apron around her waist and a big smile on her face. "Can I help you?" she asked as she walked toward me.

"Hello, yes, I'm Lizete, and I'm hiring a yurt for the week."

"Oh yes, welcome," she said. "I'm Silvia."

My heart softened and all fear released. I had been guided here. I could see it in her eyes, and I felt it in my waters. She showed me around the farm. It was a glimpse of paradise, so different to what I had been building in Costa Rica, but so similar in intention. There were two domes, distinct in their use and style, and more than ten distinct yurts on different levels, each perched on their own individual porch. Permaculture and nature were honored through different cultivated gardens, and a beautiful lake sat in the heart of the farm. You can tell when something has been created in love.

After the tour, I met Arthur. I learned he had built this place based on a vision with his beloved. She had passed three years before because of cancer, the same disease that had taken my dad, and I could see it in him. He was a man lost without love, and my heart broke for him. But he welcomed me warmly and took me to my simple, yet homey yurt. It had two single beds, a light duvet, and a little nightstand. Outside, it had a lovely porch that extended just perfectly under a beautifully leaning tree. I was delighted. This would serve just fine.

As I lay in bed that night, I realized it was March 2, 2022, Ash Wednesday. Although I'd spent twenty-two years within the Christian church, this was the first time I'd paid attention to the first day of Lent. It signifies the beginning of a forty-day period (around six weeks) of fasting, contemplation, and setting things right with the divine. This was the time Jeshua was led to the desert before His ministry could begin. I was ready to reconnect with all of me and all the divine was ready to reveal. I wondered how we would get along. Me and my higher self. And this community. *Time will tell, as it always does,* I thought to myself, as I gently fell asleep under the night sky and the dome that would be my home for now.

For the next seven days, I pondered deeply. With space and time to focus 100 percent on what Spirit was saying and what my body was communicating, I became attuned to how my new environment and community served as a sacred mirror simply to observe, completely unattached. Each day I would listen to the meditations I had prerecorded for myself. Although I had been leading retreats and sacred sessions for other people since 2012, I had never guided myself.

These meditations opened distinct gates of consciousness and chakra centers that I now use within my Genesis retreats for others. I was guided to tap into my true self—the self that existed before my birth or identification with the name I was given. Before I knew the rules of what it meant to be a "good girl." Before I had been conditioned or had labeled myself anything. It was a clean slate and, amazingly, the very first week I had ever given myself the time and space to be true. Eating only when my body requested, sleeping when needed, and interacting as I was guided. It was a breath of fresh air and a complete rebirth. Just within these seven days, the distortions became crystalline clear as I met myself with no conditions in love for the first time.

There were many tears as I realized just how fragile, small, and delicate I was, and so many laughs as I saw how the exact opposite was also true. I knew my infinite nature, and sensed the power and presence of the moment of now. I had rebirthed, just as Spirit had promised. Seven days and seven nights to create a whole new world.

My new world was created through my own awareness.

THE POWER OF THE ESSENTIAL ECOSYSTEM

What can makes this multidimensional process somewhat heady and hard to grasp is that it is a three-in-one process. It is a journey of inner personal leadership (awareness). It is an excavation of hidden treasures of forgotten innate power (activation). And it is a healing journey (alignment).

So, what are we really healing? I have found that it is *confidence*. When we have clarity on our calling, confidence is our natural state; however, we have all been through circumstances that hurt this confidence. The effortless confidence and open curiosity we are innately born with is lost as years go by and our educational system (as well as societal norms in general), tells us that we don't know what we are doing and that things should be a certain way.

It is a journey of layers as we peel back the moments, events, and words that crushed our spirit or shrank our natural creative resolve. We have been trained to be small—but we were not designed that way. We each have a sacred soul that is infinite, and all we really need to remember and embody is that we bring everything we need within us when we arrive. We are more than intelligent, enough because we are intelligence itself. We are more than beautiful enough to be loved, because we are each the expressed image of God in individual form. Yet that is not how we feel. This is the programming and separation from our source. This is what we are healing in truth, each for ourselves.

You may have heard the old phrase, "You come with nothing, you leave with nothing." Well, I'm here to demonstrate that this is a lie. We come with everything we are, and we have the opportunity to come into this life and make of it what we wish. It is all down to the confidence of being oneself. Within the ARISE Academy, we focus this understanding within time and space, as this is the most practical way to apply this consciousness and understanding. As we let go of the paradigm of survival, which says, "I need to be someone and do something so that I get to live," we step into surrender.

When I discovered this, I stopped pushing, forcing, and imposing my ideas on creation. Instead, I could lean back and observe what was showing up effortlessly, who was choosing to listen and understand, which opportunity was the path of least resistance. When we start learning to flow with the stream of source, we realize we have tapped into the immense power that truly does bring everything into fruition naturally.

So, what is there for me to do? Well, my part. My free will in having the confidence to say yes, and to say no. This is multidimensional mastery, as we confidently flow and operate in a new certainty of support and safety. We are attuned to our higher self and aligned with our power to take the step we feel in our heart. We learn to open our mouth and let out song, not because it is perfect but because it is perfectly felt and true. We harmonize our air and our waters in our physical form. Our essence expressed.

Confidence is natural when we feel safe and sound. This is our work as leaders within our own individual healing. As I heal the spaces within me, I no longer need validation and confirmation from outside of myself. I only entertain individuals who stand with me, with no need to convince or depend on those who do not. This is our journey of healing within the Essential Ecosystem, and I hope that it delights you, dear one. This is our divine inheritance if we choose to claim it. This is our freedom to move through space and time with conviction and confidence. Without it, we are constantly anxious as the whirlwind of change and chaos moves seemingly out of our control. Indeed, we cannot measure confidence by control; that is a trap. But when we know we are safe in clarity and calling, confidence is part of the being that emerges and is reborn.

So let us break this revelation down.

- **Air/First Dimension/Authenticity:** YOU. As you are. A seed. A spark of light. A sperm. Nothing can be added, nor anything taken away. You are whole and complete as you are.

- **Water/Second Dimension/Mother:** Received you as a seed and provided you fully with the environment in which you naturally thrived. Your body is the seed growing, not separate from the full intelligence.

- **Earth/Third Dimension/Identity:** Once you arrive as a human being, you are given a name and forget the Mother's waters. This is where the false ego is born— from the very need to survive. We are on our own and need to be someone and do something or we won't be able to pay rent or function in society.

- **Fire/Fourth Dimension/Transformation:** As we cultivate the burning and purifying flame of love on the inside, our relationships serve as a mirror to see what was hidden or obscure. It is sharpening us if we will see the lesson. If we will love the vessel. If we will own the feelings and the results as Spirit's guidance. It is alchemizing our lower-frequency grief, apathy, guilt, and hidden shame.

- **Space/Fifth Dimension/Embodiment:** Here, we embody who we really are, not who we think we should be. We are not meant to be some "ideal" that someone else has imagined but who we actually, genuinely, wholly (holy), and authentically are.

RECOGNIZING THE CONFIDENCE IN YOU

There was a night I should have left. A moment when everything was shown before it got ugly and beyond repair.

Nathan and I were sitting by the fire, relaxing in beach chairs, and listening to the jungle. Our dogs were around us, and I looked over as the fire flickered across his face. Nathan was moody and distant again. Detained in the prison of his inner thoughts. And then he stunned me.

"Lizete, I love you so much. But I'm not in love with you. That's the only reason I am not into making love. I could sit in your presence for the rest of my life, and I love your company, but you don't turn me on." He took a breath. The night never sounded so loud as it filled the void. I couldn't breathe. "You're just not my type," he finished.

I could tell that he had been preparing and thinking about this for a while. My heart beat wild and crazy in my chest.

Was there anything more frightening that these words from the very man I had faced every fear of snake, scorpion, lizard, and frog just to be with?

"Not your type? Didn't you think about this before you asked me to marry you?"

He looked at me curiously. Oh, he still wanted to marry me, he clarified. He loved me more than he had ever loved anyone, it's just that he didn't want me physically. Desire is one of the truest compasses there is, and it was what had been used against me up to this point. He had said over and over: it was not me, it was him. And though I understood, that could not be enough for me. I wanted love, not company, and knew I would not be reduced to that. I had spent two and a half frustrating years investing in someone who told me they loved me twenty times a day while subjecting me to mood swings and gaslighting me and not treating me with any dignity. How had this happened?

Within the seemingly endless silence, my heart screamed.

It was in that moment of deep anguish and despair that I saw the field. The easiest way to describe it is like I was looking at a shimmering wave. Spirit was showing me life force. I could see energy for the first time in my life and it was like a womb. I could see the waters that surrounded me. I was shown that the story he was sharing from his experience was a projection of his consciousness on me, and I was being shielded from that. It had nothing to do with my worthiness or desirability as a woman.

While he had been expecting resistance, once I had this revelation, all sorrow disappeared and was replaced by joy. I understood instantly that Spirit was with me, and I was still in the Mother's womb. I was not his type, okay. He couldn't change that—so, finally, I had the freedom to let go. As I did, I felt relief, my life force immediately returning. He witnessed the shift of consciousness and the joy and love that ensued in me after that channeled information. Intrigued and curious as always, he then seemed to change his mind.

He professed his unconditional and unchanging love for me. What he'd said before had just been a moment of insanity. Of course I was his type, I was his twin. There was no one else but me ... and on the story went.

That is the moment I should have left him. I knew Nathan had spoken his truth the first time. I was in a situation that was not good for me. I should have known that what he wanted was information about what I knew and the fruits of my gift. He wanted to be with me for what I had to give, but he didn't love me as I was—not completely, anyway. If I'd had the confidence—if I had known my strength and the value of my presence—I would have left then. This is the Ecosystem versus the ego and what it thinks it needs to survive. The conditioned mind. Within real love there is no need for sacrifice or alteration. I had settled for an empty acknowledgment that didn't give me safety, benefits, or even just the pleasure of someone who loved me.

The work of the Essential Ecosystem is to separate the illusion between words and actions, our hopes and our reality. The result is crystalline clarity. May we be loved for who we are and not only for what we have to give. What emerges is the you and I that are arising, dear one. We are the emergence of a whole human being.

The greatest gift of this relationship was the clarity that my calling is indeed to give my all-in love and service to my partner, my family, and the world I am here to serve as my whole and true self, for I cannot be anything else. I am here to love my God and love the other, as well as to be free and loved for who I am.

If I had just had the confidence—if I had known my innate worthiness—I would have simply packed my bags the following day and gone. But I didn't have the confidence I have now. That needed to be cultivated; it needed to be healed. When we build our confidence, we no longer need to be victims of other people's whimsical needs. We have the strength to understand and accept others while taking steps in peace to secure our own life. We must learn to see the lines in the sand.

PART II: ACTIVATION

The Heart of Alchemy and Sacred Service

I have come to believe, beyond a shadow of a doubt, that the supernatural, universal field is unconditional and perfect love. It has been my faith and my devotion to co-create in my experience to the best of my knowing.

It is written: 1 John 4:8: "The person who does not love does not know God, because God is love."

This was confirmed to my very core again during the seven magical days of my retreat at Enxara. In spite of my deep grief, the community embraced my presence. Arthur and Silvia both invited me to stay after my seven-day fast. "Stay at least for three months," Arthur said, welcoming me and my dogs to the sanctuary.

The invitation came upon the heels of a very beautiful and magical ceremony I did with Arthur. I explained my leadership model to him, which is based on the idea and research that love is the only commodity that multiplies. Then I played my crystal bowl and sang the songs that had been coming to me in my innermost chamber of worship.

He was blown away as he felt the presence of the love open through the portal of his heart and mine. Once we finished, he embraced me and asked, "What is the point of having it all if we don't share it?"

That is indeed the question in these pivotal times. We as the human population have the real commodity—love. Love is who we are in our truest nature.

Arthur and I stood at the doors of the dome his late wife had imagined and constructed with him, looking over the majestic hills that surrounded the farm. The buildings, garden, lake, and cabins. Indeed, a sacred place that still held their love for all to feel. Their love held me in my healing from heartbreak.

True wealth and health are in the honoring of our gifts and

finding our way to create harmony. This is what we are cultivating in this second pillar of activation. We are activating our sacred service. What is that one thing that you have to offer and contribute to the world, that is so valuable because it is simply unique and authentically you, Empress?

CULTIVATING EMPRESS ENERGY

After a rapid three-day visit with Mom to pack some more essentials, I sorted some boxes with my books, studies, and office equipment. Back at Enxara, I was set up with two yurts and would work in one as an office, serving the community and furthering my research. The second would be my sleeping quarters. The meals were absolutely delicious, and I felt spoiled by Silvia's warm, nurturing presence. Each day there was a new thing on the menu, and I was free to come and go and eat as I pleased. We grew closer.

The following three-month experience is one I will forever treasure. It was a moment in time that I was living in a space rent-free without needing to pay for anything, fed three meals a day without cooking, and simply honored for existing and doing the work that came to me naturally. To have the opportunity to truly discover and cultivate one's multidimensionality is a rare gift. The transformation I was able to cultivate is exactly what we will be diving into in these next chapters. This would become the origin experience of my Three-Month Essential Ecosystem Experience. This is the coaching program at the core of the ARISE Academy.

In my research, I found humans can complete our soul's purpose in this plane because we carry both masculine and feminine energy within. It depends on if we can cultivate divine masculine and feminine within us, even if we have never received it externally.

The Empress knows who to give to, when to give, and how to give from abundance without overextending or depleting herself. She moves from wholeness and fullness. This is when you are a channel. This is activated Empress energy, and if this is what you are longing for, I now call it the Essential Ecosystem Experience.

The structure that Spirit had guided me to revealed what was required for the human soul to heal. This same structure was used as a guideline for designing every experience within the Academy. We have already briefly outlined this, but I will define this critical understanding here in order to go deeper.

Air/First Dimension/Authenticity

YOU. As you are. A seed.

The primary reason that these three months of my personal Essential Ecosystem Experience were such a healing and transformational experience, allowing me to purge the first fifteen kilos of weight, is that there were no demands or expectations on my time. I had the freedom to be completely where I was and how I was as time unfolded. There were days of deep grief when memories or melancholy would arise, but then I would rest and have the space to honor that transmutation.

Other times, I would have a boatload of energy and harmonious company available to share it with. There was a natural rhythm of giving and receiving that I had not yet experienced. The ego was not required here. There was awareness, and the primary focus was on myself and my healing. I was free and loved for who I was. Maybe for the first time in my life.

Now, I run retreats for other people who desire to spend sacred time within themselves, and it is one of the things I most love to do as a container of transformation. It may feel daunting to simply take time away from what has already been established within your life, but a retreat is something you can always give yourself. A moment to pause, relax, feel, reflect, and make some new decisions.

You are the seed that makes everything happen, so please don't ever be talked out of taking time and space for you. Everything you need for your life is already within you and has always been patiently waiting for you, however it is up to you to choose to make time for it. This was the secret I uncovered that I wished someone had told me. But then again, we are only ready to embrace this when we are willing and ready to hear it. I hope you hear me, beloved, because you are worth every moment of your life—but maybe like me, you have never been affirmed in that.

Water/Second Dimension/Mother

Within the second dimension there is a duality and counterbalance that makes this structure work. There is firstly authority, a clear leader who holds the yes and no. Each person knows their place and serves from their unique capacity in their authority. The second power is acceptance. This is the feminine principle, more subtle and easily missed.

For all personal authority we abdicate, we automatically accept the decisions of others—and the outcomes that follow.

This is a powerful revelation. To understand how to calm your waters emotionally, there has to be leadership that is kind, safe, and fair. For me, this meant a leadership I could trust while owning my own leadership and personal responsibility. This is truly the internal process for each sovereign human being.

We each have the decisive masculine energy in the physical to navigate and the infinite feminine energy that is informing us about our surroundings and field, inside and out. She senses and knows in her waters and all he needs to do is listen closely. Choose wisely.

Earth/Third Dimension/Identity

I was reborn. Awakening to this new person I was experiencing. Remembering what it is to actually be free, as myself. Breathing at ease, safe and sound, with time and space to integrate all the new revelations from within my chakras and allowing.

Yes, actually putting my devotional faith to use for the good of myself. Surrendering. This was so new. So fun and exhilarating. The changes that emerged were so beautifully easeful and yet so profound. ARISE was no longer an acronym I had channeled. It was not just the name of my five-day retreat. It was becoming a way I could understand Spirit speaking from within.

As we anchor our infinite potential in the now as a multidimensional master, we require harmony in three areas: the three pillars of the Essential Ecosystem:

- **Awareness:** The Soil, Carbon, The Mental Body/ Masculine Free Will Deciding Energy

- **Activation:** The Waters, Crystalline, The Emotional Body/Feminine Multidimensional Energy

- **Alignment:** The Light, Physical Human Body/ Manifest Illumination Energy

The physical body was the most surprising for me as I worked out this Ecosystem. The two primary things I did were rest as much as I could and remove five key things from my nutrition intake. We will dive deeper into the food-specific guidelines I used in the next chapter, as that is quite a conversation on its own. But I would like to share here that I was not dieting at all, and yet, within three months lost fifteen kilos and over the following year lost thirty kilos. Not only did I lose the layers of excess weight, but I also regenerated my physical body with curves I didn't have at twenty-one and continue to enjoy a vital force not common for anyone over forty.

All in total freedom.

I accomplished this based on an understanding of food as frequency, as well as transmuting the main metaprograms of what I had subconsciously accepted as the speed and rat race of "normal life." This is the actual cause of much of our dis-ease.

As I was setting myself free mentally and emotionally through the ARISE process, I was nurturing and nourishing my body in peace and freedom. While I healed the stress, my body naturally healed itself. I chose to remove everything that creates inflammation and the weight I had carried for the last two decades simply melted away.

Fire/Fourth Dimension/Transformation

This element is where the rubber hits the road and things get real. The fire element is alchemical work. Where we turn the lead of our lives into pure gold. The spiritual and supernatural energy is the refining fire that cleanse everything or burns the house down so we may build anew.

Much of my transformation happened in sacred ceremony, deep meditation, or with the support of mushrooms and a shaman I trusted to hold the space. These are ways to join with those who are already connected to planetary consciousness and the natural world. Much of this feminine and natural power has been demonized by the overculture, but my gifts started coming online, I knew I had these abilities.

I sat with Spirit in one such ceremony and asked, "Who am I? Am I a shaman? A mystic? A channel? A wayshower? Am I a medium, Lord? Do you know the people who say they love you burn people like this?"

Spirit, ever so gentle and loving, whispered, almost with a slight giggle, "You are sacred, beloved. You are sacred. Everyone is sacred." And indeed. The element of fire within our Ecosystem teaches us, each in our own way, that every experience, person, and moment is a perfect co-creation born of free will. They will either serve for our destruction or for the building of character and wisdom. Spirit walks us through the fire: Are we committed to things that are using and burning our energy? Or are we using our life force to build effectively and productively for the good of all?

That brings us to the work of the fourth dimension. The element of fire purifies all bodies as we walk through the three pillars:

- **Awareness**: Building CLARITY around our CALLING and healing the inner conviction that produces our incorruptible CONFIDENCE.

- **Activation**: Conjuring the COURAGE of the heart to authentically express our natural CHARISMA that magnetizes the CONNECTIONS needed for our unique calling.

- **Alignment**: Nurturing and cultivating the CONSCIOUSNESS that serves us as a guiding light. To remain COHERENT in the ways of COMPASSION and Christed Consciousness.

This is the transformational process embedded in this book, and also the twelve-month journey and twelve-step process of the ARISE Collective. Each of us walking, growing, and evolving side by side.

Space/Fifth Dimension/Embodiment

In 2014, I bought a golden bikini that I never wore. It was too small, and it was very expensive. It was a whimsical want. Still, I bought it in faith that one day, I would wear it. I kept that bikini in a drawer until the end of May 2022—my graduation day of the Essential Ecosystem Experience. I not only put on that bikini, but I felt and looked better than I had ever known myself to feel and look.

I was not only comfortable within my own skin and free in my peace of mind, but the work was showing in the glow and beauty of the body that was emerging.

I always knew my mother to be on some sort of diet. Growing up in a household of three or, at times, four women and one man, the conversation was often about beauty and wanting the body to change in some fashion or other. There was not one diet that ever made my mom lose weight and keep it off—until this method, which is not a diet. It's a whole experience, a new introduction to what is actually possible with the human body. In the next chapter, we will go specifically into which critical foods are needed to purge, cleanse, and calibrate the body.

Today, it is my deepest passion to support people into deeper love and health with their bodies. We recently graduated our pioneer students of the Essential Ecosystem Experience. One of them sent this feedback: "I have transformed beyond my dreams and continue to do so. I feel free, empowered, and confident in myself, my abilities, and the choices I make. I can give to whom I want to and receive when I'm in need. I can speak my truth. My heart is grateful to you and to ARISE."

I have never had a prouder or more fulfilling moment in my professional career. This showed me that not only were these results possible for me, but they were replicable for others.

We heal ourselves. We heal our mothers. We heal others. We heal women. We heal the world.

This is the pathway of activation. This is the pillar of sacred service and the unleashed power of the divine feminine within each person, regardless of gender. However, I now specifically speak to women leaders: There is so much nonsense that we have heard about our bodies, and it is time to set things to right. Our body is the apex of creation and the most valuable commodity on the face of the Earth. Every war that is fought is on the basis of wanting to control others because our very bodies are an energy source.

That is exactly why, beloved woman, we are called to ARISE.

We need to show the way. As leaders, as mothers, and as role models. We want our sons to be living productive and happy loving lives, not like Nathan, a soldier who was lost to the trauma and damage of wars fought for things he couldn't even justify to himself. We are here to end war. Within and without, in the name of the whole. In the name of women. In the name of humanity. There is no need for it when we already have everything we need to return to and co-create Everyday Eden.

So, activation is about understanding our health (the expressed vital force within our vessel) and our wealth (the value we can give and receive). We do this by honoring and excavating our ancient and future individual gifts, which we can only do if we take better care of ourselves.

Through this Essential Ecosystem you will rediscover what it means to truly return to a sovereign state. What is that one thing you love to do? That you naturally do and would do for absolutely nothing every day? Maybe it's not just one thing. Indeed, it has taken me the last two years of piecing myself back together and finding ways to honor and serve my gift, myself, and my clients. We have been sold a lie that making money is stressful, yet this is not what the Ecosystem has shown. The better and brighter I am, the more my business flourishes and the more value I have to offer to others.

So again, I ask you, dear one, what is that *one thing* you have to offer and contribute to the world, the thing that is valuable because it is unique and authentically you?

Courage is beckoning. It is time to face the unknown.

ECOSYSTEM FOR EVERYDAY EDEN
Energy Flows through Dimensions

First Dimension	AUTHENTICITY		
Second Dimension	AUTHORITY	ACCEPTANCE	
Third Dimension	AWARENESS	ACTIVATION	ALIGNMENT
Fourth Dimension *inner work*	Clarity Calling Confidence	Courage Charisma Connection	Consciousness Coherence Compassion
Fifth Dimension *the result*	SOVEREIGNTY	SACRED SERVICE	SECURITY

(DIVINITY WHISPERS)

I love you beyond time and space.
In this and every dimension. In every lifetime.
Thank you for doing your work. Being faithful to us.
I admire you greatly as a human.

Your devotion and commitment to an ideal
is beyond any human potential I have met in a person.
Firstly, in building our home.
Secondly, in remaining faithful to me
in these times of seeming impossibility
that there is anything left to wait for.

Use this, my love.

This devotional POWER OF LOVE that YOU ARE.
Let it be your strength.
Never let it be your prison of stubbornness,
which is the shadow.
You are the most beautiful and tender being
under the sheets, whether cotton or steel.

*Be quick to forgive. Be quick to let go.
Be quick to laugh, my love.*

*Your smile lights up my WHOLE WORLD AND UNIVERSE.
I love you. And no, these are not final words or a suicide note—
but if I don't get the chance to tell you how I feel—
now you know.*

CHAPTER FIVE

Courage: Stepping Into the Unknown

Courage has always been one of my favorite words. To be brave and courageous is one of the highest attributes of our humanity and rightly awarded to the best and most valiant of souls. Courage is the highest frequency in the third-dimensional plain. Unfortunately, like all naturally divine frequencies, it has been gravely distorted. Too often, courage is coupled with sacrifice, loss, or death—like soldiers throughout the ages, lost to the conquest of war.

Yes. I knew this courage. I admired it greatly in Nathan, my retired and moody soldier. He had courage—but courage like that will always lead to destruction when not harmonized with higher love. We need a redefining and restructuring of our most potent "weapon" and "tool" so we can learn to use courage to build life instead of sowing destruction and chaos. We need the courage to create peace.

This is exactly where Spirit led me. There is nothing more courageous than deciding to be who you really are. Nothing and No Thing. Courage is different than confidence because, even though we now have the clarity of our calling and the power of our awareness, this next step takes us into the unknown. Tension, presented as some sort of fear to overcome, is what creates the need for courage.

For the masculine side, this is a great fear of failure. For the feminine side, it is the fear of the mighty unknown. What happens if I do this, what happens if I do that? For both sides, anxiety is born in the deep despair to lose what is loved, what is cherished and precious. We are afraid to make the wrong choice at the crossroads and can become paralyzed, waiting too long even when it seems the decision is made for us through circumstance.

During my three months at Enxara, I had the space and time to practice awareness and build its momentum like a muscle. Instead of a reactive survival mode, I was in a reflective creative mode. This was the conscious choice made every day. That awareness led to my activation, the first step of which is finding the courage to take that first step.

A NEW WAY TO FOOD

While I was working with my mind and emotions through meditations, songs, and channeled transmissions, my new battlefield was the physical body. No matter how much we rework the mind and the heart, the physical body is an equal and needs to be nurtured and nourished so that it can cooperate with the evolution we are discussing.

When it comes to our bodies and what is healthy, the first thing people generally think about is dieting. I have a personal disgust with dieting because I watched my mother on the hamster wheel of different diets my whole life—and I wasn't immune. I tried, hoped, got frustrated, and felt terrible about myself. Even when something worked a little—at great cost—the weight all came back anyway. Diet was the dog chasing its own tail, and I was done with it. Diet is a path of restriction. The journey I invite you to, beloved, is one of freedom.

But in this new space and mindset, I started to remember that I am not separate from my body. In truth, the body is still in the Mother's waters (the universal field), responding and reacting to what we create in this field we are immersed in. A loving understanding began to develop that this beautiful, organic, incredibly intelligent creation was ever present, ever faithful, and ever hoping to serve me. My body.

I had never consciously been aware of my body like this. Previously, I'd seen it as a tool to get things done, and to get me from here to where I thought I needed to be.

I was guided to remove certain things from my diet. First, I want to be sure to tell you every single item removed from my nutritional intake came back into my regular diet within three to nine months. My weight has been stable at a very comfortable and healthy fifty-five kilograms for the last year. We are meant to live in abundance and eat, drink, and enjoy every good thing, but how we consciously think about it and how our body is calibrated to digest and distribute what we ingest to our cellular structure is the whole new playing field.

I am not a nutritionist, but I am a foodie. I absolutely love food, and the most precious moments enjoyed in the jungle with Nathan were often centered around the kitchen. We planted food, collected food, made food, and ate our mothers' favorite recipes together. We planned to write a cookbook honoring the precious meals and memories of our mothers, each bringing our own delicious recipes to the table. I learned to love to cook, and it filled my heart like I never knew possible. Just watching him eat was a thrill. We ate well in the jungle, but that book was not to be.

In truth, I enjoy these meals still, but my body processes them differently. In just three months I knew I had reprogrammed my DNA to digest and receive food differently. The layers of excess weight I had accepted as part of normal aging and my sedentary lifestyle were actually the trauma of a lifetime operating within a lower matrix. That was all. I was not broken. I was not old. And neither are you.

When given the right conditions of love and the right vibration of natural divinity, our bodies start to operate in an aligned, high functioning, natural healing state. The weight I lost has never returned, and for the last two and a half years, I have continued to refine, rejuvenate, and surprise myself. How I was able to transform my body using this understanding was based on the revelation that love, and our divinity, is experienced differently in each of the bodies.

Let's take a look at the things I initially cut out of my diet.

- **Alcohol (Air/First Dimension/Authenticity)**: The first thing off the menu was alcohol in any form. This meant wine or spirits of any kind. On a journey of consciousness, we are stabilizing our mental body. Remaining sober and contained is critical to this experience. We need to be clearheaded to know what is real, safe, and true. With the mental instability I was experiencing, alcohol would have only led to dependency, addiction, or violent texting that doesn't look good on any soul. So, booze had to go.

- **Dairy (Water/Second Dimension/Mother)**: The next thing on our list is milk and all dairy products. This is specifically because milk creates mucus in the gut. There is nothing I love more than my morning coffee with two sugars and milk, but for three months I removed milk so my gut and my waters could become clear. Giving my body this opportunity allowed the vessel to cleanse, and I could feel and sense my true emotion so much better. Milk and dairy products are also often polluted with all sorts of hormones, which greatly affects our natural hormonal balance. Removing dairy for just three months was better for me than any hormonal replacement therapy I had ever heard of.

- **Processed Foods (Earth/Third Dimension/Identity):** There are a lot of artificial things in our food these days, and sugar gets a lot of heat. I found it's not really the sugar that causes havoc. Our body needs sugar to function. The real culprits in processed foods are the artificial, unknown ingredients that the body doesn't have a map to process because they aren't natural. The body either can't break down the alien ingredients or they are causing harm to the cellular structure of the body. As I removed all snacks, sweets, chips, and artificial food, I felt for the first time what my body does naturally. This reprieve also broke any unconscious addiction or dependence on binging junk food. No more emotional eating. Instead, I would eat fruit, nuts, and healthy snacks that did not confuse my natural regeneration.

- **Bread (Fire/Fourth Dimension / Transformation):** This was the hardest for me. Bread was off the menu. As such a fundamental piece of our everyday lives with snacks and sandwiches, this is a hard one for many. But the gluten in bread is problematic. Even if you don't think you have an intolerance, the quantities in normal bread literally poison our system. Although it won't kill us, it enough to put the body into a state of defensiveness and out of its naturally healing alignment. This natural defense creates inflammation. The body is not wrong. It is doing its best to keep us safe. It was incredible to me to see that a lot of the thirty extra kilos I had been carrying around for twenty years was inflammation and not fat as I thought. Thankfully, bread was the first thing I was able to add back into my diet within three months.

- **Meat (Space/Fifth Dimension/Embodiment):** Being born and raised in Botswana, meat was the primary element of my meals before this transformation. Meals were built around the choice of beef, pork, or fish. Meat, of all of these elimination foods, is the densest frequency and that is why it is vital to cut it out. Removing animal products was a stretch for me, but in practicality, once my mindset shifted and I didn't need to figure out the meals, I honestly didn't miss it. The most powerful revelation I received through removing meat was to appreciate my own flesh. My own body as well as the animal who had dedicated its life to be my meal. It would take me nine months to reintroduce meat to my diet. When I did, I noticed I was much more mindful and concerned about where the meat came from and how the animals were cared for.

Note: Please take this all as it applies to your values and ideas as I share this roadmap. I love animals more than anything and yet I also know that if we didn't eat them, we would not breed them. It's the chicken and egg story, if you will. Today, when I do eat meat, I source consciously, buying animals that have known a long and full beautifully free life. The better they have lived, the better the frequency I will be ingesting.

Chapter Five — Courage: Stepping Into the Unknown

INTIMACY / COURAGE
Five Things to Change

AIR ELEMENT

Mental Body

Spirits + Alcohol

SPACE ELEMENT

Soul/Light Body

Meat + Animal Products

WATER ELEMENT

Emotional Body

Dairy Products

FIRE ELEMENT

Energetic Body

Bread + Wheat + Gluten

EARTH ELEMENT

Physical Body

Processed Foods

AN ENCOUNTER OF DESTINY

Now, let's look at what happened next for me on this transformation, connecting the idea of changing your mindset about the temple and body you are inhabiting.

Things were in full swing at Enxara. Dynamic, peaceful, and

productive. I was sitting on the coach in the main house enjoying a tea after a lovely dinner, when the most beautiful and elegant lady strolled in. She was absolutely charming and warm as she greeted me, explaining she was hosting a retreat for the next three days and looking for the receptionist.

"Yes, that would be Silvia, and she's expecting you. I'll get her for you. I'm Lizete," I said, shaking her hand.

"Thank you," she said sweetly, introducing herself as Sophia. "Are you a retreat leader too?"

"Yes, I am, but for now I'm here doing a healing retreat on myself."

She was curious and asked if I would be available to join her and her partner, who was flying in from Brazil the next day.

I was delighted, and it felt incredibly cool to be invited. "I'm happy to bring my singing bowls with me, if you would like," I offered somewhat nervously.

"Absolutely!" she said. "Looking forward to seeing you then."

The next morning, I sat in the dome in a circle. The participants arriving, each getting a yoga chair and taking their place. A tall, beautiful, dark-haired man walked in and immediately I knew this was the partner from Brazil. Henrique had presence and was clearly attractive. I remembered when that potent combination used to stir me to the bone. Now I felt nothing. Absolutely nothing. Surprising.

The workshop began, a discussion about the nine archetypes of the sacred geometry of humanity. Even though I had never studied it, I understood it implicitly. It was another portal of understanding about how to develop our consciousness. I was right at home. It was also nice to sit there, listen, and be served, and the group was willing to venture deep and share from the heart.

It was just after lunch when the Henrique came toward me.

"Dear Lizete, are you willing to play your bowls to open the afternoon session?"

"Of course, yes, I would be honored." The miracle unfolding.

I sat in my place in the circle, the bowl in front of me. I began. The bowl song rang around the dome and then I closed my eyes and started to sing and open the field. About five minutes in, I opened my eyes. The whole room was in deep stillness and immersed in the music. Henrique was watching, mesmerized, and I could see his hands shaking as he held up his phone, filming the experience.

I was surprised and taken aback for a nanosecond. Was this okay? I could feel the ancient insecurity. Yes. I was more than okay, and he had just never seen the field open and move quite like this. He was a studied yogi, an athlete, and a devoted teacher. He was also the son of a medium who had served for many years, and he had seen much of the supernatural world of healing. A world that I had never had the privilege to see. He saw me so clearly, and in his reflection, I started to see myself.

By afternoon, the group was fully formed into a harmonious and relaxed band of brothers and sisters. A participant called Nigel came over during a break. "I love your dog. She's amazing."

"Thank you," I said. Sami always served with me on private retreats. She would run up to certain people for cuddles, seemingly at random to the untrained eye, but I knew she was on to something. She had repeatedly visited Nigel, who was quite touched by her persistent, loving attention.

"You know, Lizete, I think you are so cool, but I don't know about any spiritual stuff. I think I'm what you would call a skeptic."

I nodded. "I completely understand, dear one. Please don't change a single belief on my account. I'm just visiting." I smiled at him, and I smiled within myself.

I had come to feel that there is nothing to believe except what Spirit is sharing with you, and it is not my place to convince any sovereign being about anything. I liked my new peaceful and contained approach. It was liberating. I was just being myself. Having the courage to be myself had given me an inner comfort to just be where I was and accepting everyone else for where they were.

After the break, the retreat leaders asked me to sing again. I began a new song, opening up the higher dimensional fields, and I could tell that the participants felt divinity fill the room. We sang, receiving a channeled message and the healing we needed. It was truly glorious. There was a moment during the guided meditation I looked over at my new friend Nigel. He was standing straight, his hand on his heart, eyes closed, and tears rolling down his face as he received the transmission. I walked over to him and placed my hand on his. His eyes opened and met mine.

He smiled the biggest smile and said, "Lizete—it's only love. It's only light."

"Yes, dear one. You are deeply loved," I replied with tears running down my cheek. I was touched and honored by the honesty, courage, and vulnerability of this beautiful being.

"Oh my God, what I was expecting I don't know, but it's so beautiful." He had felt the love of Spirit. He had felt his own divinity, and I had my answer. There is nothing more precious in the whole world to me than seeing a human being waking up to their divinity. Seeing it. Knowing it. Feeling it. Reconnecting with the source, their unique source.

It is one thing to commit to taking care of yourself. And it's another to know why your presence and contribution is important to others in this life. The balance to authenticity is to love God and to love another, which means my gift automatically has to be creating a benefit for someone or something else. This is the balance of sovereignty and sacred service.

You, dear one, have gifts as well. Some you may know very well. Others may still be hidden from view and buried under labels and layers of separation and forgetfulness.

MOMENT OF TRUTH

In the evening, Sophia and Henrique had organized a ceremony around the fire. I had been with the group the whole day and didn't want to impose, so I decided to excuse myself. As I was sharing this with Henrique, Nigel overheard.

"Oh Lizete, you have to come," he humorously pleaded. I laughed at his affectionate open and charismatic gesture. He had gone from being afraid of my presence to loving my presence—and what a difference that made. Well, okay then. I guess I was going to ceremony. Nigel insisted on carrying my bowls.

Henrique gestured for me to sit at the head of the fire, he took his place beside me. He had never drummed in his life, but that night we were beyond the mere mortals we had known ourselves to be. After an initial opening, I asked him to play the shaman's drum and the rhythm of it was intoxicating and my feet seemed to have a mind of their own. The whole group uplifted and connected to the night sky and all her beauty. The fire and its alchemical magic reminded us of our inner flame just waiting to transmute all the brokenness in life. I danced and danced and danced. I moved in ways that my body knew innately, and I had completely forgotten.

As I sat, I felt a message wanted to come through and instinctively the group calmed down. We grew quiet and still as we listened. The words came.

"You don't know yourselves," it began, and I was shocked. *You don't say that to people*, I could hear myself think. Yet there was complete surrender and trust in the voice of Spirit that I had allowed. This was the one to listen to.

"You don't know yourselves. You know your experience. You know your life and your desires, but you think that you need to be this one thing. You are not one single thing, beloved. You are what you represent in every moment. The choice is yours."

I felt pure relief flow through the group. The forgiveness and love of Spirit poured out upon us as we were freed from all guilt, shame, and grief of everything we had carried there to that alter, until that moment. We were free to create. To choose again. To decide for ourselves what we represented. It is incredible how the stories of life inform our identities and although we have one name, we are ever changing. The person I am now is not the being I once was, yet I am still myself. This profound revelation would carry me deep into my journey.

The last day of the retreat was upon us. Henrique and Sophia asked me to participate in the afternoon, where they were teaching about the Enneagram. Basically, they introduced the archetypes and discussed how, when we position certain people to play certain roles for us, we connect with hidden emotions and subconscious programming. I knew I had been cast in the perfect role and open to see what Spirit was going to share with me. I was loved and held by this group, and I could feel something big was coming.

Henrique was guided to put me in the middle of the circle and called a man to stand behind me. I could feel the masculine energy in him. He felt needy. A little too quick to please. Not strong enough to catch me. He was nice enough but didn't do anything for me. Then he placed another man in front of me. This man was very strong and very wounded. He started shouting at me. He started spewing all the anger, hate, hurt, and grief in his soul. Yes, I knew this masculine as well. So well. It was not comfortable to be in that energy, but I was surprised how I could tolerate and take it. Then the angry giant did something I was not expecting.

He started seeing something shining above my head. He placed his hand on my crown with curiosity, and the minute he did, absolute white-hot rage erupted from my sacral and root chakras. I grabbed his hand, pushing it off my head and shouted back at him, stunning him into silence.

"Not behind me! Not in front of me! Not below me! Not above me! You are supposed to stand beside me!"

The words literally sizzled out of my lips as I was seething in anger. Henrique was at my side, whispering, "In love, my sister. Can you say it in love?"

Woah. Love? Say it in love?

After this treatment, this abuse, and how he'd tried to take my divine connection, steal my treasure? I breathed deeply, my body shaking. I looked at Henrique. I saw a man who had guided this retreat for three days with absolute grace, poise, and professionalism. As devastatingly gorgeous as he was, this was the first man I had ever witnessed who didn't use his sexual energy to seduce, sway, or impress. He was contained. Whole. He encouraged no flirting and dismissed seductive attention outright. I looked at him and said, "For you, brother. For you, in honor of your excellence."

I turned back to the raging warrior who looked like a lost child at this point and said, with as much love as I could muster, "Not behind me. Not in front of me. Not below me. Not above me. You are supposed to stand beside me. Side by side."

He fell to his knees. His arms desperately pulled on my waist as he wept apologies and buried his face in my stomach. I stood there stroking his shoulder and head assuring him it was all okay. And then I saw it.

As I lifted my eyes from the wounded warrior on his knees, Henrique's eyes connected with mine. I could see the light in them staring at me. *He sees me.* Tears rolling down his own face. Standing right in front of me was the most ideal man I could have ever imagined. He was perfect for me as a partner in every way. The love exploded in the room. I wish I had stepped away from the wounded warrior and just run into his embrace, but I couldn't move. Maybe he had not seen what I did. The exercise ended.

As everyone packed up and was leaving, there were many tearful and emotional hugs of gratitude. I supported this group for three days and they had experienced a better retreat for it. I was content and so were the leaders. I went to Henrique, and it was just us. I sat in front of him and shared what these three days had meant to me. I told him of how broken I had been, but how seeing a man of his caliber showing up restored hope in my heart. I appreciated him not flaunting his sexuality or his obvious attractiveness, and he started to cry.

"Why are you crying?" I asked gently, wiping the tears from his cheeks. "Am I saying something wrong?"

"Not at all," he sighed. His lips were inches from mine. "I have waited for a woman to see me in this light my whole life. To know me and trust me. To understand my mission to work without any jealousy."

I understood. This man's faith was solid. There was nothing this man was going to do that wasn't Christed. May I also say his conviction was the sexiest and hottest thing he had going on? I could see it, clear as day, and what a turn-on.

"When I looked at you, I saw the very ideal partner for me," I shared shyly.

He laughed and said, "Likewise! That is exactly what I saw."

Wow. He was leaving, and I was just getting to truly meet him. Oh, what is a girl to do.

"I would like to see your work sometime, your leadership model." He blurted.

"Wonderful. I would love to show it to you, but you're leaving."

That day, he traveled to the north of the country to spend time with Sophia and her husband, and in hindsight, I'm so glad he went. That night as I lay in bed by myself, I wondered why I hadn't embraced him when he cried. I had done that for everyone, but I had not shared affection with him despite the sexual energy and chemistry between us.

I would have my answer in just two days.

THE COURAGE REQUIRED

Henrique was going back to Brazil but wanted to visit with me for the morning before catching the flight. I was excited for his visit; however, when he arrived and we actually connected, although friendly and lovely, it was not the same. It was not Him. And I was not Her. I knew it and he knew it.

What showed up in the field was a lesson about what we each represented. I needed to see the level of partner who could see me as The One. And he needed to know that there was a woman who would honor his excellence and trust his word. There are men who truly deserve that, and he taught me that too.

We were healing each other. Each walking each other home, in the famous words of Ram Dass. It's amazing how, in the field, you see something that is so real and then you need time to see what is really, really, *really* real, right now. We are walking through time and space, beloved. Walking with the divine requires discernment. It requires courage. It requires a gentle but powerful surrender without attachment to the knowing that what is arising is for the best of all. This is difficult to believe at times, yet it has been proven true, time and time again.

I was so glad that I was not attached. I didn't fall into the dreamlike state of romance and fantasy. I was strong in my Ecosystem with the ability to wonderfully and plainly remain on my own. And now I knew that the most handsome, honorable, and beautiful of men would then be able to see me.

I was never to see my handsome Brazilian Henrique again, but we had already given everything we needed to give to each other. The promise of love was made to both of us. Each on our separate journeys.

I knew, that day, I would remain single. Single, and singular in this one focus of my life: to serve humanity with my song and channel frequencies and vibration that supports us to transmute the density that blinds and binds us. My partner, the one for me, is known by my Mother. Is known by my Father. Jeshua called the divine "Abba." Yes. As above so below. Abba would guide his steps to me, just as every one of my steps was being guided. I need not look. I need not despair. Love will find me. I just need to represent.

Love is not fabricated or manufactured. It recognizes and it remembers. My partner, my one, will find me when the time is right. This is a sweet promise I feel filling my heart.

It took courage. But it was ever so worth it.

We are worth it. You are most definitely worth it.

Matthew 6:22 says, "The light of the body is the eye. If therefore

Chapter Five — Courage: Stepping Into the Unknown

thine eye be single, the whole body shall be full of light."

Shortly after this encounter, I was sitting one day in my yurt and a new song stirred in my heart. I was preparing for the next leg of this odyssey. The three months were up. My time at Enxara was ending.

While listening to the Dixie Chicks, I saw an energetic bridge open, a portal in the astral, and started to spontaneously travel at light speed. Out of my body I flew, right across the Atlantic Ocean. I saw the Costa Rican jungle, the farm Nathan and I had built together, and I flew right into the house. I hovered above the bed that used to be ours, and I saw Nathan lying on the bed. He was staring at the ceiling. Lost in thought. I hovered above him and said, "I still love you, silly." Like I was answering some question he was pondering. "I will always love you. But now my love is free. My love had to be set free."

Instantly I was back in my body, in my yurt. I didn't know how I had just done that, but I felt deeply that I had just received a key to heal my grief. My love needed to be set free. Tears coursed down my face. But how unjust. Why did I need to lose the one person I loved most to share my love with others? Well, simply because with him, I wasn't allowed or able to be myself. To him, I wasn't enough as I was, and he made me feel it every single day, whether through curt criticisms or by outrageous gaslighting stints.

I had learned. I had truly loved. I felt now how I wanted to be held. Freely. As me. Any other kind of love would just not be real enough. I started noticing how the love Nathan and I shared was still intact. Even though I couldn't kiss his face or hold his hand. Every person I met was now getting to feel, sense, and know the love that had been. The love I was and still carry.

A divine love that is true for every human heart that is courageous enough to be willing to receive it.

We as humanity have been conditioned relentlessly that we are not enough. That we are too much. That we are somehow broken. That is the lie and conditioning we are overcoming within ourselves. For me, as a woman who loves a man, this has meant that I have to be appealing enough to hold his attention for eternity. From everything I experienced in this life, including with Nathan, that is Mission Impossible.

In truth, it is up to each and every one of us to use our attention as we wish in free will. For myself, I had to learn that if I was good enough for me, everything else would follow. I learned that I had put way too much emphasis on the external fleshly manifestation and now saw that it is the essence that attracts, holds, nurtures, and loves. We truly only need to be ourselves, and that is the quest of courage we are on.

When you treat your body as sacred, it will be treated as sacred by others. This takes courage to understand; it takes responsibility to accept. Never again will I ever let another man touch me who doesn't appreciate the beauty, power, and love of my being. Thinking I'm sexy is not enough, and if that's all he sees, that's not enough either. I want to be valued for the sacred service I represent, that I carry in service of my clients, humanity, and the whole of which I am a part.

My partner—the one I call my beloved—needs to share more than my bed; he needs to share my heart and my mind. We need to be on the same mission. No longer do I look on outer appearances to know the truth of soul. I only need to see what people pay attention to and what they choose to express.

It takes courage to know what I am willing to fight for and that I choose peace above all else. Love. Love is what I choose—joy, peace, and enlightenment.

Chapter Five — Courage: Stepping Into the Unknown

This is the choice within me, and within all of us. This is my free will.

This profound insight connects to food because of the simple phrase we often hear: "We are what we eat." Though perhaps it would be clearer to say, "What we eat may separate us from who we really are." As you nurture yourself, you give yourself a whole new worth that shifts every relationship, every dynamic and circumstance in your life.

In truth, people treat us as well or as poorly as we allow. They do not have to change—we need to have the courage to embrace love for ourselves first. The next time I see the eyes of love staring at me, I promise you I will run toward them. Remaining stuck with a crying, wounded soldier hanging on my waist is not my destiny. Just like food, partnering with others requires courage to know ourselves and honor our own needs. Incredibly, I have found that this creates the charisma to attract the exact people I truly want to be connected to.

And that is our very next step.

(LIONS GATE TRANSMISSION)

Will we listen to the inner whisper of divine mind?
Sacred soul, purified body.
Will we listen with ears to hear?

Do we not realize only truth will set us free?

Yet we cower in the corners of Shadow
for fear of what we will hear.
If you only knew how deeply you are loved.

How perfect you are in the sight
Of Father God. Of Mother God
of your sacred family
that longs with a deep ache to know you again
and to be known by you, beloved.

Do not hide in the corners anymore.
Come, come, come into the circle of love
where you are held,
where you stand in the light.

Do not be afraid of the truth.
The truth will set you free.
The truth of you ...

will only ever set you free.

CHAPTER SIX

Charisma: The Art of Living and Loving as You

"So, what are your next steps right now?" my friend Maria asked.

We had connected during the retreat I had supported with Henrique, and she was back attending another. Again, I had been asked to sing and serve as a part of the leadership running a three-day experience. I willingly served the retreat group.

"I need to write my book," I said. "I've learned so much in these last few years that people need to know. I need a place to be completely on my own and just to write. A sanctuary in nature. That is my next step." I had the insight and conviction. I just had no clue how I would actually do it or where I needed to go.

To my surprise and delight, she turned to me and said, "I have a sanctuary for you."

"Excuse me?"

"Yes, my family has a farm in the Alentejo—Sao Pedro de Corval. No one lives there at the moment, but secretly I hope it will be used for exactly the kind of work you are doing in the future. I hope to be like you at some point, spending my time supporting and guiding people through their healing."

"Wow. I don't even know what to say. I'm not earning anything right now," I said sheepishly.

"Nothing is needed. If you would like to use the house, you can use it," she said matter-of-factly.

"Why are you offering me this?" I asked, truly curious.

She took her time, feeling deeply and then said, "Lizete, what I felt when you sang the first time and every single time since, is a feeling that I have always been looking for. A knowing of something so deep within but that I haven't experienced in the rest of the world or in this lifetime. I remembered your song in my soul. I know I'm meant to learn from you."

We closed our conversation with the agreement she would talk to her husband who co-owned the property and would get back to me in a couple of days.

The next step of the journey had shown itself. Everything in me knew that this is what I needed to do. And it came about because of the power of charisma.

A NEW UNDERSTANDING OF THE LAW OF ATTRACTION

Charisma is your natural energy. It is the most magnetic and powerful energy we can embody. It is what creates the magical star quality that one exudes. The secret sauce that separates the leaders from the followers.

I have always had a keen awareness of this particular energy in others. For fifteen years in my corporate career, as I traveled the world meeting faces in new places, I noticed almost immediately who had charisma and who didn't. As I observed and studied this phenomenon in my personal life, and also in leaders and celebrities on the world stage, I noticed that each person who had that it-factor was unique, specific, and consistent. The single thing that was universal was that they appeared free to be themselves.

They moved through the world deliberately, as if they belonged wherever they were. They said what they wanted to say and didn't doubt the words coming out of their mouths. They had an ease that others didn't.

Charismatic people are sure of themselves, and yet it is more than confidence. It is a knowing and presence they emanate, and it can be felt by everyone witnessing them. Charisma is not about being nice or pretty. Rather it is about being real, clear, and even raw. At its most beautiful, however, it presents itself as grace. Grace is the nature of charisma. Calm. Comforting. Assuring and focused. It is not boastful. It is not higher than anyone else. It is not impatient. It has time—much like love.

Most women develop the ability to shapeshift as a skill to survive. There is plenty we think, feel, and want to say, yet as we navigate the world, we constantly adjust and adapt to the room we have entered. This is a mastery in itself; however, for women specifically, I find this to be the great imbalance we are healing. We adjust and accommodate and morph so much that we lose sight of the fulfillment of our needs or are in so much pain we are callous and unaware of the needs of anyone else. Charisma—like every single aspect of our journey—is a question of balance.

Everyone in the corporate world talks about "work-life balance." I've attended talks and courses where the instructors gave structure about dividing time and compromising, yet in truth, this is a fallacy. My work is my life, and my life is at work every day. From the multidimensional perspective, it's truly about the energy one has in every passing moment. I am not ready to write at every moment; sometimes, cleaning the stove is exactly what I need to be doing. This is where balance is truly created.

The lower matrix has been organized to ensure that you don't have time to find a balance that works wholly and purely for yourself. The matrix itself is not a physical thing, although it is very real. It is the structure of time and space that we co-create as a collective. The process I share with you now through consciousness is to navigate time-space reality with higher awareness that is not only higher in frequency but also true to our natural divine template. We have collectively been programmed since a young age about what time we need to get up and how much time we must spend at work. We work in jobs that define what our time is worth. We are constantly running after arbitrary deadlines and ensuring that everyone else's needs and wants are met before our own. That is a trap, and it has disempowered us all.

This leaves us lost in the future, planning something while we are actually deeply unsettled or unresolved about the past. The conscious and unconscious are battling it out, creating a war zone for our consciousness instead of a warm, safe, space of creation. This creates the imbalance or instability that we are not in the right place at the right time. This is not how the feminine or masculine operate in wholeness.

Whenever I have met a charismatic, powerful person, they know where they need to be, and they show up with all their presence. For so many of us, the only reason we don't feel more powerful is because we have been split into different roles—daughter, mother, partner, friend, woman, professional—instead of realizing we are all these things at once. This is not multi-tasking—another abused fallacy. The human mind needs to focus on one thing at a time, so being whole means that I am in complete peace with what I am focused on right now and that it is exactly the thing I need to be focused on for the good of me and the whole.

As much as I am here to contribute and give of myself, I am

also here to receive, rest, and enjoy myself. Our essence and that which we co-create with our soul and spirit can only be found in the silence and stillness of our own voice. How are we ever to create this Heaven on Earth we feel in our hearts if we are too busy to listen to ourselves? So often when signing on a coaching client, I know our work will be untangling this imbalance.

Remember this: You are naturally charismatic, beloved.

No single individual is like you. You are the most beautiful version of you that will ever exist. You deserve all the love and attention. And no one is going to give it to you until you give it to yourself. That is the key lesson of charisma.

LIKE ATTRACTS LIKE

When you are confident in who you are and following your calling, your charisma comes alive. It attracts like-minded individuals who can support or serve the mission that is imprinted in your heart and known by your soul. When I connected with Maria, singing the song she always hoped to experience, I was just singing. I wasn't looking to connect with her in particular, I was not trying to impress and didn't realize any benefit for me in our connection. By simply and wholeheartedly offering myself and my gift freely, I had touched someone with authentic expression, and it literally opened up a house to continue my journey.

Through this type of authentic charisma, I attracted other faithful companions to join me on my evolutionary journey. Each week, the ARISE Collective met on Thursday evenings to learn the new insights Spirit had given and address questions or concerns. This forum served as the place where we evolved together side by side, navigating the process and lessons I'm outlining here. This unity and community have been a lifeline to everything I have co-created.

Just before I was to leave Enxara to go to my new sanctuary in the Alentejo, a natural and more rural eastern province of Portugal, I invited the Collective to spend a weekend and do a retreat with me. Hanne from Norway, Valerie from the United Kingdom, and Carla from Portugal joined me, all excited to finally meet each other in real life. They were thrilled and surprised at my physical transformation, which they hadn't fully been able to see on Zoom. The weight had been melting away and I was different, inside and out.

I first met Valerie at a women's circle in December 2020. After the loss of her husband, she dove deeply into personal development and leadership training, but had burned out on the trainings and courses, feeling that she had plateaued, that she wasn't learning anything new. But like Maria, she too heard my song and knew I could help her. Though she had decided she was not investing in any other course, she felt called to work with me and signed up for a six-week experience I was running called Women Leaders ARISE.

Valerie had been on her own journey and wasn't quite sure how to voice what she was looking for now. After a childhood riddled with hearing and health issues, solitude in school, and abuse at home, she had chosen to dedicate her life to become a nurse. Like me, she was compelled from within to be of service to humanity. After a fifteen-year career though, she'd had enough. Though she tried her best to help people, it became increasingly clear that health services were more focused on the bottom line than the patients' needs.

The work no longer resonated. I could relate. I'd had the exact relationship with the pharmaceutical industry.

Val then swerved, starting a successful international cake baking business with her husband. But after he passed away, the business became too heavy, and she again had to dig deep and find the strength to begin again. She did. She built her own health and wellness center in her home and trained to become a licensed NES health practitioner. She became interested in bioenergetic scanning, which tests and reads the frequencies a body emits and focuses on healing the mental, emotional, physical, and energetic bodies.

I loved her approach and knew I could help her. What started as a coaching journey became a friendship and then a business partnership combining her bioenergetics scan with my transformative alchemy of transmutation to offer a qualitative and quantifiable way to track progress on the healing journey. This was the birthing partnership of the ARISE Academy.

On retreat at the Enxara farm, we felt again how right this connection was and how we were naturally in sync and in flow. We were discovering how we could put our work out into the world. Though we had two very different points of view, we were united in our common and universal objective and tools.

Feminine energy is magnetic. There is no reason to flaunt or perform to have real charisma. This has been the distortion of some of the abuse of charisma we have seen. Things that look slick and perfect on the surface can turn out not to be real. The charisma we are cultivating here comes naturally. The more you become your true, real, and authentic self, the more your charisma will shine through, attracting those who genuinely appreciate and accept you for who you are, as well as *where* you are, through it all. Valerie has been through this entire journey as a faithful and loving business and soul partner indeed, and that requires truth as the foundation and throughout.

We all naturally attract the exact match of the frequency we are emanating. As your frequency rises, so will the qualities of the people that surround and support you.

WHO ARE YOU WHEN YOU'RE ALONE?

With the help of a few friends and a grateful coaching client, we (my dogs and I) were able to move to the new sanctuary in the Alentejo within a few days. Known for its ease, nature, and wonderful food, the Alentejo was a place I had only visited twice before. I had no idea how this was going to unfold, but I trusted my steps. I trusted the one guiding me ever onward.

I arrived late at night, just past eleven. The drive up to the farm was absolutely magical. The moon was full and bright and seemed to guide me on my way, whispering sweet nothings, as the wind blew in my face. Full of energy, and so excited, I unpacked the car, put things in their place, and gave a few treats to the dogs, who had been excellent on the two-and-a-half-hour drive from the coast. I settled into my new bed for the night, surrounded by acres of space all for me. A beautiful country home with everything I needed. My heart was full as I felt into this new place that would be my sanctuary.

Having the time and space to do what we are meant to do in this life is the very definition of freedom. Until this moment, I had been a fish measured by how well I could climb a tree. Well, game over. I knew what I was meant to do now from the inside out, and nothing and no one was going to tell me differently. A new lesson was emerging. I was learning who I was when I was in the presence of no one but myself. And I really liked her.

The next morning, I walked out into the garden with my coffee, and I felt at home instantly. The sun was still low in the sky, and it was a beautiful warm morning in June. I had arrived at the beginning of the hottest season, but I absolutely loved it. It reminded me of Botswana, my first home, my roots and where my people come from. The chickens and ducks who lived on the farm greeted me

Chapter Six — Charisma: The Art of Living and Loving as You

in their beautiful language; a friendly neighbor from the farm next door would be over shortly to feed them and show me how to do it. I loved that I got to care for them in their big, beautiful henhouse surrounded by an orchard of orange trees.

I was also in charge of watering a bountiful vegetable garden during this dry season. There was a well on the property, and although it was very different, I couldn't help but feel nostalgic, as it reminded me of the farm I'd built with Nathan and left behind. Once you have known space and nature like I had for two and a half years, it is what your body and being longs for. As I walked into the fields that surrounded the property, I saw the most beautiful willow tree. It stood completely on its own in the field and it took my breath away. Willow trees have always been a personal favorite of mine, with their size, beauty, and melancholy. Loneliness suddenly washed over me, and I craved the life I had known. The man I longed for within my being. My heart was heavy and broken. Without the buffer of the community at Enxara, the loneliness was clearer, and I knew this was an invitation. Would I dare to grow stiller? Could I be quieter in the silence?

To end up alone or be alone had truly been my greatest fear my whole life. Now that I was alone, in the silence and in my new body, I found that I was experiencing and knowing my own presence for the first time. Getting to know my true energetic signature for myself. This was very new. It felt so peaceful and joyful. Some days, the feelings of grief would come up. Though these feelings were deep, dark, and intense, I had the space and alchemy to allow and process them.

I started to sing. Songs I had loved forever—from Louis Armstrong, Etta James, Sam Cooke, Barbra Streisand, and indeed all the greats and iconic artists—started flowing with an ease I had never known. I was not performing. There was no one there. I was *connecting*, feeling each word, each intonation. These were songs that understood. These were seeds of love that understood peace, joy, and enlightenment as well as chaos, destruction, and death. I was free to cry and laugh—or do both at the same time. I allowed my tears to flow freely. I was learning to be free.

Charismatic people have integrated their authority in full acceptance of who they are. They are clear about where they come from and where they are going. Though not perfect, they are not trying to be something they are not. They also remember the dream and seek a way to complete it. This is their guiding light in justifying to themselves how they spend their time and with whom they spend it.

UTILIZING THE TRAINING GROUND

After a few weeks of this rhythm of simply meditating, cooking, walking, singing, and being alone in my own presence, I was delighted when a good friend, a soul brother named Roy, called me. He wanted to come and visit with his eighteen-year-old son. I was deeply touched that he was insistent it was important, and I welcomed the company. You don't tend to feel very important while in hermit mode.

On the day of their visit, after a beautiful lunch, Roy asked if we could meditate and open the field. Of course we could, and I knew the perfect spot. Even though it was over thirty degrees Celsius, under the shade of that willow tree it was always the temperature and breeze of pure heaven. That would be the spot to go. I collected my crystal bowl and a picnic blanket, and together with my guests and the dogs, we made our way to the tree.

Once we set up everything just right, I began. Gently and slowly, I opened the field and invited them both to relax and receive. After this initial opening I then asked what it was that they most wanted to know. This was the big why of their visit. The question that haunted and lingered within the soul and compelled them to find me. What they said delighted and surprised me.

Roy said, "I would like to know where I come from."

His son said, "I would like to know where I am going."

Two generations, side by side, with the exact same questions, in opposite directions of time. How incredibly interesting. We turned to Spirit. I began to sing and allow Spirit to guide me and immediately I was shown a tree, much like the one who held us now in her loving embrace.

Through meditation I guided them into the field, to the tree and into the tree. We entered the roots; we traveled down through the many layers. Earth, rock, crystals, minerals. Layers and layers until we came to this underground cave with a lake of primordial crystalline waters. The temperature was just perfect as we were guided to step into the waters and immerse ourselves, washing ourselves clean. Where we come from and where we are going appeared to be the exact same place. To the heart of the Mother. To the divine waters of the original plan and design. It was breathtaking.

When I guided them back to the state of everyday third-dimensional consciousness, they both were reborn and refreshed. When it came to the questions "Where do I come from?" and "Where am I going?" the answer was to Mother. To the remembrance that we each come from her waters. That we will each return to her Earth. Wherever we are to walk and wherever we are to go, we are made of her and from her. This Mother is the one that holds us, provides for us, and protects us—if we are connected to her.

It was a very profound and powerful visit. I was deeply grateful for all they had brought up into my awareness. Thanking them both for the visit, I was left to my own company once again. The flow of days into evenings and music into silent contemplation along with simple farm life was a healing force. It would be a few more weeks before Spirit would reveal the next part of the puzzle.

REMEMBER WHO YOU ARE

It was August 2022, and the Aquarius full moon in all her beauty and glory literally woke me up. I can't really explain it except I was fast asleep when I felt someone call. I didn't hear a literal sound, but I felt it. Sleepy and drowsily, I lifted my head and looked up and out of my little round window in my room. Right in front of me, perfectly placed in the center, was the moon. She seemed to smile. I no longer doubted my intuition. I no longer questioned if it was normal to feel what I was feeling. I knew I had to go outside; she was beckoning, and I was willing to listen.

The first light was already making itself known and so the path was not completely in darkness. The moon guided me to the willow tree. She showed me the many cycles and lessons I had lived. I had indeed followed her from Portugal to Costa Rica to Alentejo. I had accepted the projection of others as reality instead of knowing my own frequency and truth. Indeed, I had not known it until now.

The moon said to me, "Feel the ground, this is your foundation. Trust me, Safora."

This is my spirit name, which I received in 2014 during my very first consciousness meeting with my beloved guide Sky. Now, I received the moon's love and knew I could trust. She said again, "Trust me and walk. Safora, remember who you are. The tree of life, planted as a seed. Safora, allow the seed to die and create the garden again. Eden."

Eden, indeed. My heart broke as the feelings and rememberings fully returned. Home. How had I forgotten? I felt the expansive field of love and the great dream of the Mother from time immemorial: she was created as a garden of paradise and still is exactly that. What had we done? I wept and wept and wept. The shortest verse in the Bible, as my dad would say: "Jesus wept." I understood so deeply.

As I sat in the moon's presence and in the energy and eternity of this beautiful moment, I remembered a dream I'd had early in my walk with Jeshua, while still in my twenties. We were walking in the desert together; I was following His lead. He had brought me to a group of people lost in the sands. They were lamenting, hungry, and desolate. I said to Him in the dream, "I know what to do." Instantly, I was in my pantry collecting snacks, drinks, tinned items, and all the ready-to-eat food I had, placing it in my backpack. Then I was back in the desert with the group, handing it out to all of them.

They loved it and received it gladly. We had a wonderful time, but soon all the goodies were gone, returned to dust. Jeshua stood there looking at me, silently observing. I had no answers for Him. I too had become poor within a very short time and was lamenting as if I had been one of them. He picked me up and said, "Follow me." Again, we were walking in the desert through the night. I didn't know how to get there, but I trusted His steady step, He obviously knew where He was going and all I could do was follow.

Suddenly we were at an oasis with high walls and grand wooden doors that secured the sanctuary. They opened as His Majesty approached, me in tow. He guided me through this sanctuary. It had all kinds of people playing, working, living, and loving. It was absolutely glorious. Everything we could ever need was there. He led me right through the garden to the other side. There was a well. He said to me, "You should stay here. This is what you are. The well that never dries."

I understood and yet I looked up to Him and pleaded. "But the people, Lord? What about the people?" My heart broke. I could hear their cry. I knew their desire and their need, for I had lived it myself. "How can I just sit here? I have to do something. I have to do something."

He looked at me. His incredible, indescribable, beautiful eyes showed disappointment and dismay. I didn't understand; He had never looked at me like this. He said, "We can only build a lighthouse. We can shine the light into the desert. Those who see it—and only those that are willing—are welcome to come." I felt the relief fill my being.

This was the dream that I recalled sitting there by the tree. The Aquarius full moon starting to slip under the horizon on the field, while on the opposite horizon, the sun's majestic light started illuminating the new day. Yes. I remembered the dream. The well and the lighthouse. Some will stay in the desert because that is their choice. Some will not choose to build Eden because they cannot elevate beyond neutrality into willingness to be guided. To honor and have reverence for the divine. To be willing to overcome the fear of the unknown.

It is only now upon the creation of the ARISE Academy—with the support of my mother and my business partner, Valerie, as well as the co-creation of the Collective—that I understand this dream in a whole new light.

The Academy is the lighthouse. My social presence and indeed all offering of my services is the work of this lighthouse. Some will love it and others will walk on by. His eyes in that dream and their concern also came into a whole new light.

I could not possibly think that I loved the people more than the

Chapter Six — Charisma: The Art of Living and Loving as You

one who had actually lived and died for them. He loved them as I did, if not more. Of course, His heart bleed for every individual who hurt in the desert, who was cast out of the garden. And I had insulted Him without knowing. I was acting as if His sacrifice, His example, and His resurrection were not enough. How arrogant of me.

Thankfully, He is grace and has indeed allowed me to build the lighthouse, to sit at the well that never dries, inviting all who are willing to drink these waters of healing. My self-sacrifice is not required, and neither is yours, beloved. I was healing this wound placed in women eons past. *My sacrifice fixes nothing.* I can only serve those who choose my service, as the last sacrificial lamb's blood has already restored the bridge to the divine. The King has indeed already been sacrificed.

That is all I can do. Be myself. I just have to believe that it is enough. Each has their own unique role to play. The only reason we have allowed charisma to become distorted is because we have bought into the lie of the lower matrix. The consistent and persistent evil suggestion that we are not enough. That we need to talk a certain way, say certain words, and be a certain size. This revolution is calling bullshit on all of it.

Specifically, we are attacked on the masculine side as not being intelligent enough. On the feminine side, we are not beautiful enough. With the Essential Ecosystem, dear one, I have discovered that humanity is intelligence itself. And once we know our Mother and can see Her beauty, once we know our Father and trust in His goodness, we can nurture the vessels that carry our bloodline, ancestry, and exact unique design. There is no other beauty we could possibly long to be. This is walking with Abba as Jeshua explained it to me.

A deeper pattern was emerging that would become a cornerstone within the ARISE Academy. I am forever grateful for this moment of coming home, which is when I was promised the partners, the people, the tribe that would come and meet me here, joining me in the garden sanctuary to sit under the tree.

You and I, beloved, are more than enough. We can only be who we are, and if we accept that, we will find others do as well. We can be nothing else—and how glorious it is to discover there is no one else we need to be.

In the third-dimensional reality, we are being trained and suggested to all the time about how it needs to be done. Every expert and every "friend" will tell you. In truth, you can only know for yourself, lest you blame another for the situation you are in. That is giving your power away. A power I was just discovering. The power of true charisma.

The Essential Ecosystem and the curriculum of the ARISE Academy are my contribution to humanity. They are how I believe things can be done in alignment with Everyday Eden.

Welcome back to the garden, beloved. It is time to reconnect and remember connection in a whole new light.

Chapter Six — Charisma: The Art of Living and Loving as You

INTIMACY / CHARISMA
The Four Questions

AIR ELEMENT

Mental Body

"Where do I come from?"

WATER ELEMENT

Emotional Body

"Why *this* dream?"

FIRE ELEMENT

Energetic Body

"Where am I going?"

EARTH ELEMENT

Physical Body

"How do I make it happen?"

CHAPTER SEVEN
Connection: The Tribe Supporting Your Legacy

Connection is the new frontier of evolution, and harmonious reciprocal relationships that produce more abundant life are our sole objective. It is not always easy to trust the process, but that's why I share the ups and downs of my own story.

I hope they help you remember the power and light that is already within you. One that knows, beyond a shadow of doubt, the sun will never fail to rise in the promise of a new day. That every day has the grace it requires to carry you through. May these words find and meet you in the dark endless night, tucked warm under the sheets and blankets where you rest in all comfort, safe and sound.

CONTROL AND LOVE

Control is opposite to love. Control strangles and contrives love because the one who is doing the controlling is in the frequency of fear. To master and manipulate the other, it also rules from a place of fear. It believes that is what it needs to make someone do something it wants. I understand the tactics, and I've had to use them myself. It was actually one of my first lessons with my beloved, Nathan.

In our first three "honeymoon" months, he was working truly hard around the farm, preparing to build our off-grid home in the bare jungle in a land where we didn't speak the language. We had not chosen the easiest of challenges, but we loved it. He'd bought the farm just a few months before we connected: nine hectares of the most beautiful, raw, and free jungle up on a mountain facing the Pacific. As an engineer, he had planned the whole house in his brilliant mind. The only guidance he needed was a sweet little model he had made out of toothpicks.

He had a foreman working with him who sometimes brought along extra help as they cleared a small part that would serve as the foundation for the home. The ARISE Academy had already been born in my heart when we met, and I was doing executive coaching and transformational retreats with my clients. The idea of inviting them to join me in Costa Rica was an incredible dream. However, there was lots of work to do in the meantime. Nathan was devoted, tireless, and driven. There is nothing sexier that a man building you a home with his bare hands—take my word for it. I was swept off my feet.

He had rented a little cabin in a neighboring town thirty-five minutes up the road from the farm, and I was at the cabin working on my coaching funnel and moving my business online. Our reciprocal relationship was clear to me. I would call the people and the clients, and he was building the sanctuary to harness and anchor the frequency. It all felt aligned, and everything was progressing smoothly.

One day, after he'd been away all day, I was in the mood for romance. So, I cooked a lovely meal, got showered, dressed up, and waited patiently for his arrival. When he got home, he was drenched in sweat and gave me his best smile as I met him at the door with an adoring kiss.

After he showered, we sat down to dinner. It was delicious, and although there was a lot of mm-hmming, we couldn't seem to find our groove. No matter which way I pulled the conversation it fell flat.

After dessert, it was clear that no magic was going to happen that night.

We sat on the cot that served as a sofa on the outside porch. We were listening to the jungle, sipping Bacardi and coke, simply relaxing together when he said, "Love, I know what you wanted this evening. I would have loved to give it to you. If you had just met me where I was at, given me the space to unwind with no pressure, I might have just been able to meet you there."

He had exposed my manipulation, which though unconscious was certainly still manipulation. It was true. I was so driven and passionate in my love that I had not even seen how my expectation and agenda for the evening had clouded my awareness of and compassion for the present moment.

What an incredible lesson. I spent all this time trying to get what I wanted instead of loving him where he was, and it had backfired. This was one of many, many lessons I learned with him that I will always be grateful for. This is where charisma and connection collide and merge. Knowing I am loved, treasured, and comfortable in my own skin while having the awareness to truly see and understand the other allows me to meet them right where they are in the present moment.

I have always taken rejection personally. Most of us do. Of course, it feels horrible. Yet, in hindsight, I see how every no has genuinely been my protection, and how not every yes has been the gate that leads to the garden. As we navigate with our higher selves and develop our Christed essence, we find that we are less attached to the yes and no of others as we heal our wound of lack.

As we become stronger in our own Ecosystem, we start observing every yes or no as a neutral sign along the way. Could we say yes to the adventure? Could we remain comfortable and confident even if things do not unfold as we hoped? Can we allow each step and each lesson to be a refinement of our discernment? As we set others free, our yes and no become more aligned.

Who we give our yes or no to does not say anything about the other person. It is an internal and sovereign thing. It is above reproach—or, at least, it should be if we truly long to live in a world that is free.

This is an important thing to understand as we navigate the field of divine consciousness. We are free, but we are not above or below any other. If we are to be free in our actions, we must set others free to take their own actions. It's challenging when we think that people aren't choosing the "right" thing, but this is the path of free will.

My highest hope is that you may be set free from the burden of thinking that there is any choice outside of you that you need to control or judge in any way. This may cost you people who you deeply care about, but if they do not reciprocate, they are causing an imbalance that is costing *you* much more than you realize. As they leave your presence, they create a void for the connections that can truly be a blessing to you and the legacy you are here to create.

As it says in 2 Corinthians 3:17: "Now the Lord is the Spirit, and where the Lord's Spirit is, there is freedom."

Freedom is the key to healthy, aligned, and loving connections without control. When we think of connection, we often think of togetherness, and it is paradoxical to hold the other in freedom in this unity. I do not say this lightly, for indeed I understand that this is not easy. How do we deeply connect and invest in connection when the other is free to walk out the door at any time? The pain of loss is the deepest in the human condition, especially on the feminine side, the part of us that tends to hold back in fear. This is exacerbated by the fact that loss is inevitable in our temporary, mortal human forms.

The key is where it always is: in the balance. The hard truth I have learned is that no matter how much someone appears in love, devoted, or true, they are always free to just walk out.

When we truly choose someone to spend our lives with as our life partner, we use our freedom to say, "I choose you." The other side of this coin is that we are using our freedom to dismiss opportunities to be with others—and this is one of the biggest, if not the biggest, decision we will ever make. Our partner affects every aspect of our life and is not a decision to be made lightly. We need to know the person, and the only way to know them is to truly be with them. We want to be sure that they are who we really want to be with and that they are also fully choosing to be with us. So, in this chapter, we are exploring reciprocal relationships, where we are equal in what we give and what we receive.

I live by this understanding today. I can only be who I am and give what I can in each moment. I allow people to come and go, and I give them what I feel to give. Although I have been disappointed at times, to this day all I can say is Spirit has never ever, not once, left or abandoned me.

We are never alone, but we need to choose our connections carefully, ensuring that there is an equal exchange of value. If I am over-giving to someone or something that gives me nothing in return, I will only betray myself. We are constantly making decisions to stay or go. That is the freedom and the balance of true connection. This is also why in the Essential Ecosystem we deal with sovereignty and our individual identity as our first pillar (our masculine aspect) before we can dive into intimacy and the sacred service of our feminine aspect. We are both, and we need to ensure that our partner is honoring both in us as we honor both in them.

DISCERNING LOVE IN CONNECTION

Everything is a reflection of our frequency, our co-creation of who we are or have believed we are. The hard thing to accept, though it seems obvious, is that we don't co-create on our own. We co-create with others, and we are dealing with the decisions and legacy that have been left to us by our ancestors, stored in our very genes and DNA.

While it is certainly true that we carry all that history, we can choose what to keep and what to transform. I encourage you to always only take things that you feel within because in truth, what you believe affects you and co-creates the reality you experience in your mind, emotions, energy, and body. This is the freedom we each have to enjoy together. Each will sow seeds, and each will reap harvest. This is the most naturally divine order of things that exists.

This is what makes connection magical, in my opinion. The free will to choose one person to spend and share life with also immediately implies the decision and consecration that I am not to share myself with anyone else—but has the other really chosen?

My entire theory was tested around August 2022. Nathan had been alone in the jungle since I left in May 2021, though we had spoken almost every single day.

"I think it's time for me to start dating, Lizete," he began a conversation one day. "The loneliness is killing me. During the day it's fine, I have the dogs, the farm, the work. But then the night comes, and I can't stand it sometimes. If you are not ready to come home to me, then I have to move on."

"Do you want me to come home?" I asked bluntly.

"I've been ready for ages," he retorted.

"And if I'm not ready, then you will just take anyone that comes along? Is that what you are saying?"

"I need company!"

"Company?"

"Yes! I have needs." His indignant defense was thick in the air.

"Do you still love me?" I asked openly.

"Of course. My love is unchanged."

I did not doubt his love for me. I had known it, felt it, and treasured it. It had changed my whole life to be the honored recipient of it. But this great love did not change the violent mood swings or the cycles of on and off. It didn't stop him being a force of destabilization and destruction.

"So even though you love me more than anything, instead of really working on yourself, you want to willingly deceive and use another woman."

"Not *use*," he argued.

"If your heart is with me, what do you possibly have to give her?"

He hung up.

I was in turmoil, wanting to know exactly the kind of man I had fallen in love with. He didn't care about our love, he cared for his company, his comfort, and his needs.

Had he been using me this whole time? It was the first time I thought this could be a possibility. I was lost. Tears instantly filled my eyes as I let out a scream of frustration and rage, but what happened next really blew me away. I was surprised to find I wasn't jealous. My rage was not caused by the thought of another woman touching the body I craved and missed. It was a sacred rage of how *my* time, *my* mind, *my* body, *my* life had been used, abused, and gutted for mere entertainment by this human who confused love for company.

Am I to be nothing in this life, even to the one to whom I have dedicated my all? I wondered. My sacred rage revealed his ego and exposed the ultimate betrayal. I had betrayed myself. I felt like a whore, while he had called me his wife. It had nothing to do with another woman. She was just the next victim to be used, toyed with until he became bored and sought out the next one. This is the distortion of the masculine in all of us—we use things, people, and experiences and treat them as common. I was so livid I could have broken everything in that house. Thank goodness I knew not to react.

In that moment I reached up to Spirit.

Go outside!

The instruction came as clear as an audible voice. Tears rolling down my face, I stepped into the garden, the sun blasting down its summer rays. I felt the words bubbling out of the deepest depths of soul and I screamed it out.

"I love you, Eva. Don't let him use you, girlfriend."

I was perplexed. Eva was the first woman, the wife of Adam—the one after Lilith, that is.

Spirit said, *Keep walking.*

I felt my steps guided and firm as I turned toward the sun. In my vision, I started to again see the field. There was a green aura to it and although I can't explain how, I could see Nathan right in front of me in my mind's eye. Sitting on his rocking chair, a frown on his face, his head in his hands. I could make him out so clearly, I could almost touch him. It was like seeing a holographic representation, but in clear three-dimensional form, although it was pixelated in many tiny fragments. I was seeing him through the eyes of my pure consciousness.

Keep walking, came the instruction again. And so, I did. One, two, three steps, past Nathan and into the auric field. The moment I walked past and transcended him, the field turned into bright golden

Chapter Seven — Connection: The Tribe Supporting Your Legacy

light. The sun expanded as I noticed it was right in front of me. I walked and walked into the sun until I stood and bathed. I had been set free.

This was a promise from Spirit: if I was willing to accept I had chosen someone who had not chosen me and then set him free, I would be set free as well. If I could walk past and turn my focus to the light of the sun—the Son—I would be guided into all truth. I wept with gratitude and reassurance.

I had never loved anyone or anything the way I had loved this man, and I had also never had a worse, more toxic, or more imbalanced relationship. It took me two years of healing to understand why. I had believed that he was the perfect partner for me because we had every potential to have an incredible life.

We both came from the SAME place. We were both born to mothers of European descent with a lineage rooted in Africa for at least four generations. Our fathers were both miners, strong and courageous men who protected, worked hard with, and supported their other colleagues. We had both gone to the same primary school and lived through the trauma of boarding school and being separated from our families. We loved nature, dogs, and the simple things in life.

We were going to the SAME place. When we connected, I was looking for a place to build my sanctuary to house the ARISE Academy so I could serve leaders and immerse them into nature on retreats. He had just bought the jungle farm. We had the same vision of the world returning to peace and harmony as he benefited from my teaching and saw how military life had left scars on him, similar to my struggles in the corporate world.

We had the SAME dream. Sitting around that dinner table, in front of the fire, holding hands, we both knew what was important to us and discovered nothing more sacred than our whole family surrounding us, eating and enjoying food we had cultivated for ourselves.

We put in the SAME work. Since May 2019 we had been working on the farm. Although the house wasn't ready, we were desperate to be permanently together to make it happen. I didn't care that we slept in a wooden structure under a plastic roof and no walls for over four months. I didn't care that we did everything by candlelight and only a little generator to give us electricity. I was with him, and I knew this period would pass. We were building.

We had all the ingredients to make it work—and yet, it didn't.

So, how come?

As the relationship developed, he started to doubt if I was the right partner for him. He wanted to commit. He asked me to marry him on day three—and yet, as much as he stepped forward, he also stepped away. There were periods when he would go silent and retreat. Mornings when I would turn around in our bed and look at him and instantly feel the door was closed.

How does one not know if you are the right partner? If they love you or not?

Love is light. It brings everything to the surface: the good, the bad, and the ugly. For anyone who has been in a committed relationship, we are challenged to see the whole person as they expose parts of ourselves we don't yet know. There are some parts of you that are truly loved and there are other parts that either threaten or intimidate the other. To stay in connection right and true is to accept that we are always learning to love and embrace new aspects and parts of the other person. His indecision showed the fragmented parts that were not aligned with our union and his personal truth. And I was completely blinded by so much light I couldn't see where I had been bread-crumbed, depleted, and emotionally bankrupted. As long as this invisible unconsciousness remained unseen, I would never be free to embody my true self. I had been unconsciously programmed to cancel out every part of myself and my gift that intimidated, unsettled, or disturbed my partner—and I couldn't see it. Balance is what we are creating with this understanding of connection. If we are to stay together, we are committed to both doing the work each individually.

TAKE BACK YOUR POWER

One morning when Nathan and I were still together, I reached a breaking point. It was after another period of silence, which then led to criticism and ended with him picking a fight—as always. I was exhausted and depleted by this dynamic. I called a close friend and fellow Leadership Mentor in the Netherlands and sat in my pool of tears explaining to her what was happening.

"Lizete, my dearest," she replied, "how has this happened?"

I couldn't understand her question. I wanted her to tell me how to fix the dynamic, to give me some understanding that would stop the cycles of retreat, isolation, sorrow, conflict and then having to forgive, make up, and restart all over again. It was a deep, tormenting, turbulent roller coaster.

She tenderly said, "You have given up all your power."

I was stunned. "What power?" I had no idea.

I had been duped.

If you are in a situation where you are invested in something working, doing everything you can to create peace and harmony, and yet nothing seems to work, then this is where you take our power back.

INTIMACY / CONNECTION
The Four Directions

Masculine Polarity

AIR ELEMENT

Mental Body
"Where do I come from?"

FIRE ELEMENT

Energetic Body
"Where am I going?"

Fear of Failure /
Desire to Be Free

Feminine Polarity

WATER ELEMENT

Emotional Body
"Why *this* dream?"

EARTH ELEMENT

Physical Body
"How do I make it happen?"

Fear of the Unknown /
Desire to Be Loved

"I'm not enough"

"I cannot have
what I desire"

"I am broken" /
"I'm doing it wrong"

"I'm not worthy" /
"I'm not lovable"

My whole life, I had been taught that true love was about giving—walking alongside unconditionally, offering endless compassion and understanding. As a woman, a girl, a daughter, I had never been taught that my power was also to step away, realize when I'm being played, and close the door. We don't want to see the person we love in that light. We don't want to accept that we have indeed been taken for a ride. So, to effectively take our power back, we need to understand the polarities at work.

Above all else, the masculine principle wants respect. It is not that he values respect above love, but he does demand that he is in full control and sovereign in his decision of who he gives his love to. This is the same as who he sleeps with, how he spends his money, how he lives his life. He is free will embodied.

Chapter Seven — Connection: The Tribe Supporting Your Legacy

The feminine principle wants love. She is willing to give her all to a sacred bond that she has invested in. It is not logical; it is not rational. It is real and raw. She is an ocean of water and will try to adjust herself, grow her patience, and adapt to the conditions needed in order to receive that love.

What this journey and relationship showed me was the clear mirror of both the power of my love and also the power of how I abandon, betray, reduce, and cancel myself out in the name of this same love.

He was never the problem.

The moment you realize this, you have the ended the war within yourself.

I was on a journey to discover the power I didn't even know I had. The power of love to co-create is everything, yet if it is not received willingly, reverently, and freely, it is reduced to dust.

While Nathan loved me in the moments when things were wonderful, he wouldn't allow the love to evolve and flow. He valued control over intimacy, and there were parts of me, especially my spiritual and intuitive power, that he was terrified of. He had broken me down cycle after cycle, telling me what he didn't like, didn't want, didn't need, testing exactly how far would I go to prove my love for him. It worked. He effectively made me a puppet. I let him. I had given all my power away.

As a woman who wants to have it all, the lesson here is simple although painful. You may think that other women are the problem. But they are not. When a man truly has committed to you, there is no other who can make him change. He doesn't have space left in his heart for that. He cannot be coerced or seduced to betray his beloved, no matter who the other may be. If he is undecided, though, then there is absolutely nothing you can do to convince him to be faithful, and every other single woman becomes and is a threat.

This was not the way I wanted to live. Nor will I ever live like that again. It would take me many cycles of healing and the work of this Essential Ecosystem, before I could truly understand the power my friend was talking about: The power to love and still choose respect for ourselves. This is the balance.

I had been raised in an understanding of 1 Peter 3: "In a similar way, you wives must submit yourselves to your husbands so that, even if some of them refuse to obey the word, they may be won over without a word through your conduct as wives when they see your pure and reverent lives."

You may be surprised to find this verse in a book focused on empowering women and the feminine principle, but once I was in love and truly respected my partner, this was as natural as breathing. There is, however, a second part to this scripture that is required for the balance to be complete:

"In a similar way, you husbands must live with your wives in an understanding manner, as with a most delicate partner. Honor them as heirs with you of the gracious gift of life, so that nothing may interfere with your prayers."

While the feminine principle has the superpower of devotion, the equally potent and vital energy of the masculine principle is honor. For us to give this unconditional love and devotion to someone, we also have to be very clear that this is the same level of dedication we are also receiving. Once we are not receiving this or if we are getting abuse in any form, we must know that we are in true danger.

This was the very word that Spirit spoke to me when everything came to a head that fateful day on May 18, 2021. I was in danger. Not only physically, as he could not master his triggers, his emotional outbursts, or his contrived passion. I was also in danger because I had devoted myself to someone who was not willing to give me anything. Not emotionally, not mentally, not sexually. I had been reduced to dust, and it was time to face the music.

The journey to wholeness, the light that I was shown on the day Nathan chose to step out of our union and date other people, was the invitation to my freedom. I didn't value it at the time. I couldn't see its worth. It only felt like death. Void. Destitution. But him walking away from me was the greatest gift I could have been given.

In truth, I have found we can't really "choose" another person. We certainly can't affirm with absolute certainty that we will love and continue to love that single person forever until we have made a solid, sovereign decision to choose love as a way of life.

The moment he started doubting if I was the right partner for him was the moment I should have left. Immediately and irrevocably. I should have respected him and myself enough to allow him to figure it out and then let me know. Instead, I gave up my life in Europe, my friends, and my work, and invested 100 percent into what I felt would be my future.

But here is the thing. If a man does not see you as The One, he is never going to give you the treatment you deserve. You will know by his treatment and reverence of you, not by his words. He had shown me everything I needed to know, and I refused to see it.

My power was the ability to choose me. To love me. To cherish me. I will be forever grateful for this union and this activation of love in my life. Equally, I will be forever grateful for the guidance to know that I am the one true love of my life. This is a love that longs to be free and shared with all who are willing to receive and re-attribute in kind. Anything else is not for me to even entertain. That is the new boundary.

This is when a woman decides her own worth. Not because of

her experience or how she has been treated. Not on the basis of what she saw at home in childhood as the measurement of normal. But on a foundation of truly knowing herself, trusting herself, and loving herself. How others treat us is *how we have allowed them to treat us*. It is just a reflection.

This feminine power is the one who permits until she permits no more. The choice to gently close the door behind her and take her love with her is the most elegant and empowering thing she could ever do for herself and the world.

Today all connections in my life are based on the condition that all of me is welcome at the table. I can only be myself. If it's too much for some or not enough for whatever reason, I have learned to immediately step away and let go. This is a golden rule I apply in relationships of all kinds, and it gives all the freedom to navigate in love and Spirit.

Allow yourself always to say yes to those who support the legacy you know in your heart that you are here to live. If they don't accept you or need to cut you down, do yourself a favor and let them walk right out the door.

I showed myself the door, and today I know that decision saved my life.

Chapter Seven — Connection: The Tribe Supporting Your Legacy

INTIMACY / CONNECTION
The Four Solutions

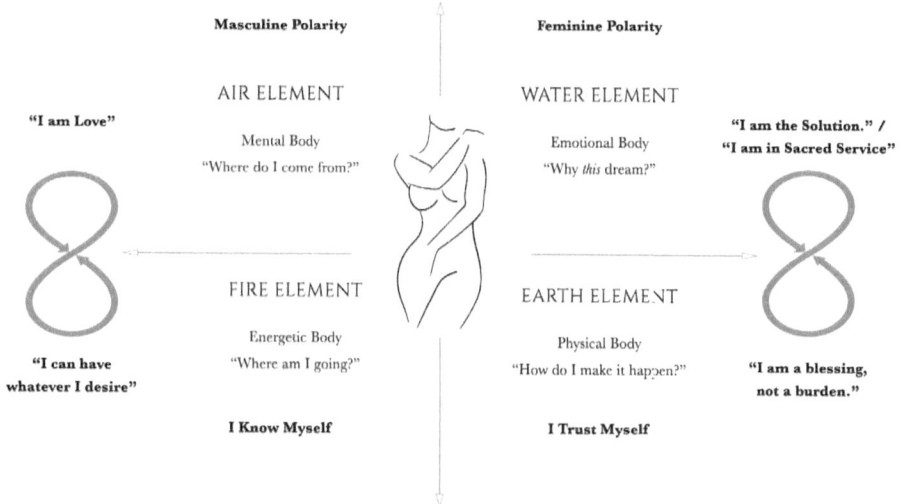

Masculine Polarity

AIR ELEMENT

Mental Body
"Where do I come from?"

FIRE ELEMENT

Energetic Body
"Where am I going?"

I Know Myself

Feminine Polarity

WATER ELEMENT

Emotional Body
"Why *this* dream?"

EARTH ELEMENT

Physical Body
"How do I make it happen?"

I Trust Myself

"I am Love"

"I can have whatever I desire"

"I am the Solution." /
"I am in Sacred Service"

"I am a blessing, not a burden."

{ 157 }

PART III: ALIGNMENT

The Power of Your Light

and Accepting All Is Right

I had been guided to this little town in the Alentejo, Sao Pedro do Corval, that contently followed a rhythm and way of life that had not changed in generations. Just the speed and stability I needed for my rebirth. Even though tiny and incredibly out of the way, it is known around the world as a center for Portugal's pottery production. Indeed, what a perfect spot to find myself. I still felt reduced to dust some days and was in the process of surrendering, just like the clay in a potter's hands.

One blisteringly hot weekend I made my way to the floating beach I kept hearing about from my neighbors. This is one of the manmade beaches around the expansive Lake Alqueva, which is the biggest freshwater lake in the whole of Europe. This was not a coincidence.

There was a deep resonance to this land that I could only sense in the energetic current. The summer landscape reminded me of the golden savanna I had loved as a child growing up in the Kalahari Desert in Botswana. It felt like home even though I didn't have any people here.

The water was absolutely lovely to swim in. Not the Pacific Ocean I had left behind, but a sweet, warm, loving embrace of ease. I could wear my gold bikini now and although I was almost twenty kilos lighter at this point, I was still a far cry from feeling beautiful and desirable in my own body.

The little Monsaraz beach bar blasted hip summer tunes and served lovely meals to sun-seeking tourists and locals alike. They had the best hamburgers in town, and it soon became one of my favorite spaces to escape to. Before, I had never been used to going places on my own, but here, even though solo, I felt less alone.

One day, content with the expansion of my singing repertoire the last few months, I made a bold move. I asked a server I had befriended who the owner of this place was. I was thinking it might just be the perfect spot to sing some tunes as a means to make some money doing what I loved.

Besides clients coming out for retreats here and there, I had not actively worked for money since leaving Costa Rica. I had been provided for each step of the way. Valerie also supported me, ensuring that I had what I needed to complete the work that I was being called to create. Her support was so vital, vast, and unwavering—that is why she is my sole business partner to this day.

The owner's name was Tiago Kalisvaart. He was a tall man of Dutch descent with a big presence and blond hair. He looked at me curiously as I walked up to him, asking if he was the owner.

"Yes," he replied, "How can I help you?"

I introduced myself briefly, saying I was in town temporarily writing a book about my healing journey in consciousness. I was also a singer, and I was curious if he was interested in live music at the beach bar.

"Yes, I am," he smiled. His sister-in-law was a professional singer and music was a deep passion of his. He was just about to take a boat ride with his guests on the lake and invited me to join them. The boat was a traditional beautiful red and black Dutch canal boat that had come from the Netherlands. It now took people on tours on the lake a few times a day in high season.

On the boat ride, Tiago served as captain, and I sat beside him so we both could share a little of our stories. He was the son of Dutch parents who were both artists in their own way. His mother, a pioneer entrepreneur who had moved to the area from the Netherlands over forty years ago, had purchased a factory that focused on weaving wool into the traditional Alentejano patterns. Her carpets, fabrics, and beautiful pieces were distributed around the world. His father was a painter and sculptor who had bought a traditional olive oil factory and turned it into a restaurant, art gallery, and museum honoring the old ways of olive oil production.

We had three languages in common, and his presence was comforting. His beautiful wife was from Catalunha, a province in Spain. They had fallen in love in college and had raised two children, now in their teens. I had found a truly beautiful family.

He played some of his sister-in-law's music, a Spanish style that was soulful as well as sweet. As we sailed on the lake, he pointed out the different features of the lake. Stone circles that were older than Stonehenge had been submersed as the lake expanded, yet I could still feel the potency of them within the waters. This whole place was something else. I could feel it and I had found someone else, raised in this place, who felt it too.

We agreed that I would come that very weekend to sing three songs. I didn't know what I was doing. I had not done it before, but I was compelled to do it. My soul friend, Roy, who had visited me with his son, was coming back with a lady friend he wanted me to meet that weekend, and I was so grateful for the additional support. Carefully selecting my three songs, I packed the car with the equipment I used at the farm, and off I went.

I set up the equipment as the guests looked on, feeling my nerves build. I was so shy and hoped they wouldn't be disappointed. After setting up, I waited for my friends to arrive, negative chatter building in my head. It was happening. This is how I always talked myself out of things.

When they arrived, I felt relieved and could focus on Roy's new acquaintance, but the distraction was short lived. Tiago came over and asked, "Ready? I can't wait to hear you." It was showtime, and his excitement gave me a boost of courage. It felt like he had opened the way. I stood up and went to the microphone.

I can't even remember the first song. I simply started, getting through it mostly with my eyes shut and finding peace within the familiar harmony. As the song ended, I was so stunned to hear the applause that ensued. I opened my eyes to see people standing up, clapping, coming around the corner to see, others with their cell phones raised as they had just filmed the performance. The second song went even better, my confidence building. For my third and final song, I'd chosen the iconic and timeless classic, "At Last" from Etta James.

As I sang the soul that touched my heart, I watched people responding to the music. Tiago off the side, sat at the edge of the terrace listening, watching the audience's reaction. I was halfway through the song when the power cut out.

I didn't understand what had happened and felt a jolt of fear and nervousness—I didn't know what to do. It was nothing too serious; the cook had accidentally pulled out the plug of the extension the system was connected to. In the awkward few seconds of silence as they fixed the issue, I looked at the audience and apologized, to which they replied, "Sing it again!" in chorus. I was delighted. The second time went even better.

I thanked the crowd for listening and packed up my gear, part of me grateful it was over, but another part wishing I had brought a few more songs. This was a massive milestone for me. My friends were brimming with pride, and their smiles gave me all the confirmation I could have possibly needed.

Tiago made his way over. "That wasn't good," he said. "That was very, very bloody good! Wow, I love your voice."

"Thank you." I felt myself blush.

"The beach might not actually be the right place for a sound quite like yours, though. I would love to invite you to perform at my restaurant in Telheiro. Would you be willing to sing at my birthday party next week?"

"I would be honored and delighted!"

That could not have gone better, I thought to myself, sitting down and sipping my wine, smiling at my friends. Something was beginning. At the party, I would be opening for another of Tiago's musician friends, so I only needed a few songs. I decided on two to honor the moment: "Evergreen" by Barbara Streisand and "A Song for You" by Donny Hathaway. I had the instrumental tracks on my computer and my favorite blue and green flowing summer dress. I was so excited to be invited to the party.

Once I arrived, I was introduced to the other artist, Quim, who went by the stage name King of Soul. Not intimidating at all. They were setting up for the band and I asked if I could do a short sound test. After, I confessed to him that this was literally the second time I would be singing in a public setting. The beach a few days before had been my first.

"Well," said King, "you could have fooled me. You handled that sound check like a pro." He smiled. I felt like an absolute fraud. I had no idea what I was doing. I just knew I had to sing, and this was my moment.

I looked across that room full of smiling faces, the wine flowing, the laughter filling the space, and took my place at the microphone. I sang from my heart and soul and shared my songs. After, a woman drew near, congratulating me and introducing herself as Tiago's mother, Mizette. We chuckled at the similarity of our names. Mizette and Lizete. Gold and platinum. She was in her eighties but exuded a grace and beauty that had not been eclipsed by age. After a couple of glasses of wine and a fabulous time, it was time to make my way back to the farm.

That night, I laid in my bed, replaying the events of the evening.

The different people I had met. The friendly staff. The gorgeous set-up of the restaurant that preserved its history as an olive oil factory while offering a cozy and comforting setting. The food—absolutely delicious. My kind of place.

I awoke the next morning to my phone ringing. It was Mizette.

"Good morning, dear," she said. "Will you be available at noon to have a cup of coffee with me at Cafe Triumph in Sao Pedro?"

"Yes, Mizette, I would love to," I replied.

"Good," she said matter-of-factly. "I think I may have a new house for you that you could rent." I didn't recall telling her I was even looking for a place to stay.

Indeed, my time at the farm was coming to an end. It was the end of the summer season and soon workers would arrive to pick the olives. What had served as a sanctuary for deep healing, as well as a place to start finding my voice and continue discovering my new abilities to channel and create content for the collective, was now to return to its owners.

After chatting with Mizette over coffee, she shared that she knew of one house available to rent and gave me the number of the lady to call. By the end of that day, without a contract or down payment, I had the keys to a new house with a garden for €350. It was only four minutes up the road in the heart of the village. I was over the moon.

Spirit had done it again. A new cycle was beginning. It was time to pack up and move once again. This time only four minutes up the road, into the village.

HARMONIZING THE BODIES

During this time, I finally had the space to buckle down and figure out how I had gotten from a place of feeling so disempowered and broken to a place where everything was so aligned and kept working out perfectly.

This is why reclaiming the feminine power to be whole and complete has been so obscured and hidden from most of us. The good news is, we don't need to have access to Catholic church vaults. We don't need the secrets of societies shrouded in mystery. We don't need to dedicate ourselves to study for years and years and years.

Although I navigated my reality as best I could, I had been stuck in the second dimension, the harmonization of the mental and emotional body. As long as fear governed my system, I was constantly stuck in the mind wondering what to do next, what to say next. *Would it be enough? Who do I have to be?*

We have the masculine principle of authority and the feminine principle of acceptance. For us to step out in the third dimension and truly be who we authentically are, we need to harmonize and balance these two. For me, shyness meant that I didn't feel safe, and the only reason I did not was because music had not become yet a part of my identity. I couldn't stand firmly in it until I saw this.

What I am about to share is the difference between the divine matrix, the space and time that we are meant to navigate in the energy I call Everyday Eden, and the lower matrix, where we are trapped in thoughts, intentions, strategies, and desires and life seems to be happening to us.

Air/First Dimension/Mental Body/ Mind of Christ

The mind of Christ was balanced in both the masculine and feminine polarities. To hear Spirit, we need our pineal gland to be clear and clean to be able to receive multidimensional information and guidance. This is the gland nestled deep within the center of our brain that receives and organizes all information.

The subconscious and unconscious mind is the feminine polarity. Most of us have never received training or guidance in how to navigate the dream space, the infinite void of our incredible right mind. This power has been obscured and only partly now starting to come to light with the understanding of neurolinguistic programming and the study of the plasticity of the mind.

It is written that Jeshua would only say what He "heard" the Father say and do what He "saw" the Father do. He was in deep sovereign connection with the divine, both masculine and feminine. When we activate our pineal gland, we have the eyes to see and the ears to hear, that had eluded me for so long. We look into other people's eyes and think they see and understand. What we must understand is they can only perceive what their frequency allows them to see, and they will only understand what is within their ability to receive and comprehend.

Water/Second Dimension/ Emotional Body/Heart of Christ

Love is the ultimate human experience, at least in my opinion. Religion would have us believe that Jeshua acted and walked like a virgin although there is absolutely nothing to support this thought. Does it not make much more logical sense that He was a fully functioning, virile, strong, sexual man? While divine, He was also perfectly human, and He too had third-dimensional desire. What He also had was *mastery over His desire*, and this is part of the evolution and development of Christ Consciousness.

Jeshua's example is one of compassion of love, but this is the not the heart that was hidden. His love for humanity and the power of His ministry to serve the many is clearly documented and known. The love that was hidden was His connection with Mary Magdalene. Mary's role has been reduced to either that of a faithful disciple or a converted whore. In my revelation of the alchemy, I've worked with both of them in personal experience, and it is clear to me that Mary Magdalene was His chosen beloved.

I wondered why the church would hide this wonderful love story never told. He was obviously on the most critical mission, and this was His first responsibility and devotion. Clearly by His side though, is his wife, always there within his ministry, kneeling and watching her beloved's death on the cross. Even in the garden of tombs it was she, together with Jeshua's mother, who was first to be shown His resurrected presence after three days in the tomb.

By removing the sacred place of Mary Magdalene, a great disservice and distortion was created. Jeshua's true example was of a pure man of singular mind and focus, who chooses one woman to be partnered with, in both the intimate and in the ministry of His calling.

Organized religion has systematically demonized sex and diminished women. The perversion is clear, and already covered sufficiently in horrid stories that continue to shock all devote human beings. The infinite terrible stories of sexual distortion amongst priests and nuns and the vile acts perpetrated against the innocent who were searching for a safe place of love is unfortunately commonplace in this time.

Paul the Apostle, the thirteenth disciple, states that he was single and celibate by choice, but also that this is a gift given to few. It is not the standard. I too have had my season to preserve, conserve, and purify my own sexual energy. Everything Jeshua taught, did and gifted us was to give us the new normal.

The love of Jeshua for His Magdalene was hidden because it

requires men to be faithful to one woman to be truly righteous. It also is the power to unlock the Christed power in a man to regenerate and perform the miracles demonstrated and promised to us all. The sacred place of Woman at his side has effectively devalued, diminished, and demonized women of all their God-given sovereign spiritual power. Please note, I am not saying that Mary Magdalene was the same as Jeshua; He is the one who brought Christ Consciousness embodied before the Holy Spirit, or Spirit of Wholeness, could be poured out upon humanity. However, even He required and was nurtured by the feminine principle in His woman of choice.

Earth/Third Dimension/ Physical Body/The Power of Christ

His enlightenment and power during his short ministry of three years was sourced by the Heavenly Father. However, He called the divine Abba. In twenty-two years of following organized religion and listening to the word of God, I only ever heard the mention of Mother Earth in the context that she is waiting and groaning for Her sons and daughters to arise. Indeed, through everything I have been shown about how the universal field works and how miracles happen within the quantum field, there is always a harmonization of the masculine and feminine.

Father and Mother God. As above so below. Abba.

The first time I ever came across the work of the Essenes, I had another massive piece to the puzzle. This was the brotherhood of which Jeshua and His family were a part, and they are the authors of the Dead Sea Scrolls. Which I also never heard about in church. Their morning meditation starts with, "I enter the eternal and infinite garden of mystery. My spirit in oneness with the Heavenly

Father. My body in oneness with the Earthly Mother. My heart in harmony with my brothers and sisters, the sons and daughters of men" (and women—my addition). This was never taught in organized religion, but it was revealed by Spirit.

ALIGNMENT / NATURAL DIVINITY
The Three Distortions

Masculine Polarity	**Feminine Polarity**
AIR ELEMENT *Mind of Christ*	PINEAL ACTIVATION *Unconscious / Subconscious*
EARTH ELEMENT *Love of Christ*	THE HIDDEN UNION *Mary Magdalene*
FIRE ELEMENT *Power of Christ / Father God*	THE CHRISTED DIVINITY *Divine Mother / As Above, So Below*

Man and woman are made to walk side by side. Like our DNA there are two opposite and equal parts. Not because we are the same, but because we are polar opposites meant to create balance. The narrative of the lower matrix has only created chaos because it has systematically canceled out the feminine in these three matters:

The power of the mind, the power of woman as an equal and relevant partner, and our great Mother who is indeed the divine manifest in form. The lower matrix patriarchy creates chaos and calls it woman. The patriarchy cannot function to its highest potential when it dominates and dismisses half of the exact template and creation of natural law.

As a woman, I was not broken. I had just never been nurtured to develop my true power. My alchemical abilities to navigate the universal field had been demonized. My multidimensional gifts were activated by accessing and restoring the feminine, while still loving and honoring the masculine. All within, as without. We in truth are just discovering what woman truly is. We are only now tapping into the true feminine power within each and every one of us as human beings.

Our very DNA gives us this picture. Genesis speaks of it: Man and woman, walking with God, side by side in the cool of the day. Two individuals devoted and committed to one another. Harmony within is peace without, and the chaos that reigns is rooted in this injustice. I have clearly seen how the war we are fighting is not outside of ourselves. It is within ourselves.

The last thing any woman wants is to send her son, her husband off to war. She wants safety, security, the sacredness of her home. The mystery is being revealed. I know what women want. They want to be the One. Just like the masculine.

Can we be faithful to one another? Our very existence may depend on it.

FINDING ALIGNMENT

I asked Jeshua once about manifesting and the law of attraction. It was in one of those low moments, and I'll never forget what He said. He showed me that we are all naturally powerful manifestors. So powerful in fact, we have manifested every single thing in our reality. Everything is our creation.

Well, I'm really terrible at manifesting, I thought, and I could feel Him giggle at me.

"No dear one," I felt Him say. "You are naturally manifesting. You are also always naturally aligned. The art of co-creation has to do with what you are aligning with."

This is the sovereign choice and the acceptance of our sacred service. As we align to the higher and release the lower, we become more filled with light. These are the choices we are to navigate in these remaining steps. Thank you for being with me so far—and hold on to your hat! It is time to unlock our independence and a new definition of security.

ALIGNMENT / NATURAL DIVINITY
The Balance of Natural Divinity

AIR ELEMENT

Mental Body
"Where do I come from?"
**God, Heaven,
Cosmic Consciousness**

WATER ELEMENT

Emotional Body
"What is the dream?"
**Cosmic Mother, Mother Earth
Planetary Consciousness**

FIRE ELEMENT

Energetic Body
"Where am I going?"
**Earthly Father, Pushing, Building
Carrying the Seed**

EARTH ELEMENT

Physical Body
"How do I make it happen?"
**Earthly Mother, Pulling, Magnetism
Holding the Womb**

As sovereign co-creators, it is up to us to create this balance within. This is what the Essential Ecosystem is designed to support us to create when we truly realize our divinity's desire and release our ego's idea of what we think we need or the type of partner we deserve.

It was crazy-making to me how Nathan could tell me twenty times that he loved me one day, yet be so confused about if he really wanted to be with me the very next day. Absolutely crazy-making. Today, I understand it is because he and I were both disconnected in different ways. He had a "type" and couldn't truly see or appreciate the person who was in front of him. I tolerated his wishy-washy behavior because I didn't think I could find someone better.

We both had work to do on ourselves.

Now that I have completed these three and a half years of transformational work, I can honestly say that there was never a man good, big, or strong enough to make me feel safe at that time. There was so much healing that I had to do by myself and for myself. While I was with Nathan, I was focused on trying to heal him. He taught me well that I, in truth, can change no one. Only the sovereign soul can choose to change, and I can support the transformation. The only thing we need is to choose and be willing.

This is a process, and in the pillar of Alignment, we will cover the next three steps of our journey:

- **Consciousness:** Truly understanding and trusting our innate power and our ability to bring light to all situations is the mastery of co-creating consciously.
- **Congruence:** While transformation is normally viewed as the process to change ourselves, this step focuses on that which is divine within you—the one that is always unchanging.

- **Compassion:** This is our final step, the leadership that is required for a balanced, loving, fulfilling, and Spirit-filled life. A new paradigm to navigate where love is more than just a word. It is the way. It is the truth, and it is the life that Jeshua referred to for all people—for the whole.

(DIVINITY WHISPERS)

I need not rush.
I need not haste.
I am have nothing but time—
eternity to waste.

I am endless and strong,
powerful and wide.
My love never ends.
It moves like the tides.

In and out,
up and through.
No point in resisting love.
It is now all up to you.

To push is to fear
that Father is not strong,
that Mother is not near
to carry you all along.
Trust, my sweet one.

You are home with me.
I will hold you close
'til it's not me or you, but we and
WHEEEE!

CHAPTER EIGHT

Consciousness: The Cornerstone of Creation

Consciousness is what I call the divine force that creates reality. Our personal consciousness is our ability to witness, discern, and understand what is real as well as what is not. It is one of the biggest and most sacred words that exists, and I was being shown how real and vast this divinity was.

I have been naturally conscious most of my life, and because it felt so natural to me, I have never understood the definitions that most scientists or experts give, normally either in terms of mathematics or physics. These were not the languages in which Spirit spoke to me, so I could never relate, and had no teachers to understand consciousness. To me, it was the omnipresence of God, Source Creator, and now I was learning how this effectively was being channeled through me and as me. I call this Christed Consciousness. It cannot be explained; it is to be experienced and known from within. This is why "remembering" is the modality of teaching within ARISE.

My gift of sitting in the presence of the divine was cultivated in worship when it was just God and me, heart to heart, communicating through song in spirit and truth. Early on I noticed that as I sang, the Holy Spirit—the Spirit of Wholeness—would move and start witnessing to others. This was indeed my calling. Yet, I didn't really understand my gift until I was guided to cross paths with a very special someone who would give me a key to unlock the door.

The first time I saw Maren was in early 2022 on an interview on the Gaia Network, where she was talking about a beautiful book she had just released. Immediately drawn to her gentle and soft nature, I could tell that her journey had been similar to mine. She studied consciousness and celebrated her gift of sight into the unseen at a time when the people surrounding me had called me delusional, crazy, or much worse. I instantly knew that she understood, and signed up for her newsletter. She gave monthly fireside open sessions, and Spirit told me to join.

Somehow, I missed the first call, but thankfully she was doing another one later that day. To my amazement I missed that call too, which was very unlike me. Something was afoot. I read through her email again and at the end there was a note that said, "For those joining me later, here is the link." I wasn't sure what this link was supposed to be for, but I knew I was meant to be there.

I joined the Zoom call, and there were only six of us. Maren began, "Welcome to week five of our mediumship program. I am curious what you have all experienced this week."

My heart skipped a beat. In the religion I'd grown up with, mediums had been labeled as demonic, yet I could feel Spirit right there with me. I was in the right place.

The students started to share. I sat in silence. I was not really supposed to be part of this group, and I was perfectly aware that she knew who her students were. I was curious why she did not ask who I was or what I was doing there. She simply allowed me to observe, and I gratefully settled in and listened intently. The stories the students started to share moved me. My eyes widened as my heart recognized everything they were talking about. They spoke of different energies of deceased grandparents visiting, sightings of pets that had passed the rainbow bridge, and many other things.

Chapter Eight — *Consciousness: The Cornerstone of Creation*

We were getting to the end of the call when she asked if anyone had any questions. When I was sure that none of her students had anything more to say I raised my hand.

"Yes, Lizete, welcome. What is your question?"

"Thank you for having me here," I began shyly. "I've listened to these stories, and I have experienced all the types of supernatural phenomenon talked about this evening. For me though, it's slightly different, and I would really like to understand my gift. I believe you have answers for me."

"Go ahead," she said warmly. "If you describe how is it different, I will try and give any and all answers I can."

I proceeded to tell her about a specific incident with a good friend, Sharon Goldsmith, that had happened during a retreat I had completed a few months back. While we were working on removing the blocks of confusion that were running rampant in her life, there was a moment when Jeshua and Mary Magdalene came into the room. I could not see them, but I could sense the exquisite and powerful presence and energy shift in the room. I asked her to describe what was happening as I sat, holding the energy but shut out of the experience. He stood in front of her and lifted His hands specifically sending light to her mind and consciousness. She described Jeshua standing a bit apart from her, ministering light to her mind, and I knew it was truth because there was no way she could make it up.

Mary Magdalene was different. She was hands on, feeling Sharon and moving things in her field to come into better alignment. She was giving Sharon straight talk, sister to sister, and again I knew it as the truth. "She's kicking my ass a little, because I don't take care of myself the way I should," Sharon shared sheepishly.

As they proceeded to work on her, Sharon had the most profound and incredible experience, despite the fact that she did not have any specific religious beliefs or connections to Jeshua and Mary Magdalene. I could see the bliss and ecstasy as she received the healing presence and profound peace that surpasses understanding.

In my heart, I was a little grieved and disappointed because I was longing to see them. I asked timidly if she could send my regards. Sharon said they smiled lovingly and said, "Jeshua says He loves you very much, and He is so glad the three of you have been working together for a very long time."

I was comforted a little, but also still confounded and intrigued, I finished summarizing to Maren. The main difference between me and the mediums in that Zoom meeting was these celestial beings and energies were speaking directly to my clients and not necessarily speaking through me. I wanted to know what it meant.

Maren's eyes grew wide in pure joy and astonishment as I spoke. I was washed by her presence of understanding and immediately felt the acceptance she willingly shared.

"That is so beautiful, Lizete, and yes, I do have answers for you. Is this the only time that you have had visitations like this?"

"No. I have had many guides that have come through to minister to different issues." Isis had made herself known during one ceremony, while Mother Mary counseled another dear friend of mine. Anubis, Archangels, as well as deceased relatives had also come through to speak, share energy, and provide insights that led to solutions.

Maren sat back in awe and took a moment. She understood, but I don't think she had met someone who actually could do this. Regardless, what she said next completely changed my life.

"Lizete, I want you to understand that Jeshua and Mary were there, and they were not there at the same time. When you go into your medium state or channel state, that is the level of frequency and energy you are connecting to. So, the person sees the individual, deity, or image of the person who best represents the frequency you are emitting."

I was stunned. "Are you saying that this is *my* energy?"

"Yes." She nodded.

"You mean, I just need to sit and surrender with that intention of service, and this is the frequency that is ministering?"

"Yes." She nodded once again.

That was the last time I would ever be overcome by fear.

This is the power of knowing oneself. My multidimensional fire was activating and purifying everything that was not in alignment with my natural divinity. I knew I had to remain on the altar and trust. No matter the external circumstances, I knew beyond a shadow of a doubt I was not truly ever alone. Seemingly forgotten by the world, I always had the most precious thing in my life. My own connection and clear access to the divine that was my source.

You, dearest one, have potential in you. If you are reading this book and searching for answers in this maze of life, then it is guaranteed that you have a gift within you. Kindness and service are the highest gifts, in whatever form your neighbor needs in truth, and the first thing you need to do is to overcome your own fear. Your very presence of stillness can, if you wish, invoke the very presence of Jesus and Mary Magdalene—or any other master.

This is the choice of working with frequency and energy. This is the mastery and journey of understanding the quantum that surrounds us and its different dimensions. Singular and perfectly attuned to each other. Taking the personal responsibility to respond and co-create our reality. I honestly believe we are all chosen. And I believe we all need to choose for ourselves. We are loved regardless. Love simply is available.

This is what consciousness has become for me. The more we choose this, the more we will uncover and evolve into these incredible gifts of Spirit, because matter and Spirit now coalesce. Harmony and rhythm with the masculine and feminine pillars now creates a third. They become one and there is no longer separation between the mind and the heart, between the left and the right. Fear is the governing disruptor, and when we can calm and soothe and create safe spaces for ourselves and others, we step into the conscious leadership that will rebuild the structures of our individual and collective lives on a whole new foundation.

It begins with me. It begins with you. We are needed now more than ever.

MORALITY AND CONSCIOUSNESS

In October 2022, I moved into my new little rented house in the village. A new experience and a new cycle of creation. As grateful as I was for this home miraculously extended to me, I noticed that it held no natural beauty. It was a typical home, and spacious, but it felt hollow and empty. Just how I felt on the inside—and so it was. It became my place of ashes and my darkest tomb of loneliness. A profound transition between the world I knew and the vastly different world that was presenting itself.

I would spend a year and three months in this void, until March 2024, when I would move again. This would be the deepest and most profound part of my healing. And it felt endless. To reclaim my power, I had to face my shadow. The revelation of the shadow and the healing of these layers would be my next step.

Where the first level showed me who I truly was, the next step was to understand what I was to create next. This level of becoming is moving in the "new" identity of who I had always been.

I never liked the silence, and had always avoided it. As a music lover and a social person, I always had people around or sound filling my space in the background, yet this was where I had been guided: to sit in the silence so I could finally hear. To listen to that still inner voice that is connected to something outside time and space. The power of my own divinity.

I was left with no responsibilities except to tend the home, take care of the dogs, and keep creating, meditating, healing and restoring myself. Laying down all responsibilities I had unconsciously carried for others, I focused on me, fine-tuning my intuitive voice and embracing highest guidance. I was doing *only* what I was guided to do for the very first time in my life. Another step into clarity. As I would sit in the silence, in the ashes of all that had been loved and lost, I found what my soul truly longed for, and I would ask two things as I sat in deep connection.

"Where are my people? What is my work to serve them?"

To start my day, most mornings I would get dressed and go to the little cafe called Triumph, situated in the town's old church square, and sit. I took the name as a good sign. I was acclimatizing to my new environment and noticed that, as the days passed, more and more faces became familiar. More people would nod good morning as I became a regular feature at the café, and they made the best latte. It was my daily treat, and the people there had no clue that this hour or two spent in the shimmering sunlight of fall would be my only reprieve from the dungeon beckoning me back.

As I softened and relaxed into the acceptance, I understood Spirit was giving me a new rhythm to walk through time and space. No need to perform, no stress, and no chaos. There was no one to tell me what to do or when to do it. There was no one to cater for, and left to myself, I had no choice but to embrace my own presence. Without having to look for anything outside of myself, I started to notice the cycles and patterns of deep moments of grief and needing to rest and cry it out. Other times bursts of joyous revelations and sparks of creation bubbled up as I continued to experience the activation of my multidimensional gifts in many different forms.

Around March 2023, spring was beginning in the village and life started budding around me. The birth of new life also brought a new friend and sister into my life and the ARISE Collective.

From the moment I met Sally, I knew there was a connection. Sally had lived in this area for six years and was originally from the Lisbon area. She loved music, and so on her very first dinner at my house with her then-boyfriend, I asked if she would like for me to sing her a song. I chose "Hallelujah" by Leonard Cohen.

The song began and filled the field. I could tell that Sally could feel Spirit, and she was amazed as tears rolled down her cheeks. She had waited for this for a long time and was filled with questions. How could I call on this presence so quickly? Who had I learned this from? How did I do it? I chuckled. I knew that I could answer her questions; however, I was hesitant due to her Christian background.

I had been educated extensively with the same conditioning and objections. Jesus, although praised and worshiped in the churches I attended, was also systematically separated and isolated from any spiritual power. The organization and centralization of His teachings meant that if anything was not explicitly just like Jesus, it must be of Satan and therefore demonized.

What I had been shown and guided to learn in the last thirteen years painted outside of the accepted boundaries according to organized religion. It had effectively locked me up in a cage. As much as I loved Jeshua, I was systematically controlled and manipulated by fear until I came to know Him as the crown energy.

The Christed frequency is pure Source consciousness, but due to fear of the unknown or the fear indoctrinated that God is vengeful, many will shun any other ascended master or teachings. I was not fearful to access, embrace, and transmute all. It was not just theory to me but an experience and a growing expertise of transmutation. Quantum physics powered by faith.

I shared a little of the story I am sharing with you with Sally, and explained that I serve as a guide and mentor. "That is what I am called to do," I said, "And I am happy to share if you are willing to receive."

She said yes—she was going through her own transformation as her romantic relationship began to disintegrate. Stepping out on her own for the first time, she recognized Spirit and had the inner conviction that we were meant to find each other. Perfect timing for us both.

"Are you a Christian?" she asked me one day, as we sat sipping our lattes at the Triumph Café.

"An interesting question I have asked myself, dear, and I would have to say yes and no." I answered. I had accepted Jeshua as my Lord and Savior because I believe and trust in the provision of His sacrifice and resurrection. My life is surrendered to Him, and all my work is in alignment with the sacred scriptures as I know it to be the living word and what works.

At the same time, all the churches I'd attended didn't accept that any human could possibly have actual spiritual power. Even though Jeshua explicitly states that we will do the things that He had done and even greater things, the centralized church is not invested in developing this mastery within the people. My gift for example, while acknowledged, was constantly under scrutiny while I was being controlled, condemned, and judged. Not much love there at all.

There seems to be no room for growth or grace in the churches I've known, though certainly not all churches are like this. But I stopped looking. I just no longer needed any external validation of my divine connection. I started to hold church within my sessions, within my community, in my recording of songs and my morning meditation. I started creating my own Everyday Eden lifestyle, really, for myself.

The compounded result of control is that though Christians consistently talk about love, they follow a set of dogmatic rules and protocols that do not allow for anything outside of prescribed, archaic ideals. This was never the gospel I believed in. I walk a path of love, accepting and loving everyone where they are, and that is all I am interested in. Peace.

Consciousness has a morality all on its own, but not all morality has consciousness. Morality predetermined by others attempts to define what is right or wrong for the sovereign individual. Then, it imposes that if you want to belong, you had better comply. We often sense or have a knowing that something is wrong, yet we go along to get along because we want to belong. This system is designed to keep us bent and disempowered. We are not meant to judge each other—only love each other. Imagine the freedom when each of us as a unique and sovereign consciousness, understands that each human soul will answer for their own self. No one else.

Let's dive deeper.

The "dungeon," as I lovingly call it—the dark night of the soul—had freed me from the need for agreement or compromise. I knew what was working for me and that was all I needed. If I was wrong, I trusted Jeshua would surely guide me in becoming aware of my error. My commitment is to Him and my own conscience.

Morality is also something that is mutually agreed upon for a specific period of time. It is timebound while consciousness is timeless. Slavery and colonialism were heinous acts performed in the name of spreading the gospel, after all. I often say that when truth speaks or enters a room, it does not require a name tag. Truth is recognizable just like love. Consciousness is dynamic and in the present moment, freeing the individual to make a call on their inner yes or no.

I am not interested in the slightest in telling others what is right or wrong. I would always be wrong if I tried. Love is about accepting the one where they are and allowing them to choose. That is the very heart of the gospel. We are loved unconditionally by the divine and in each moment, we can make a new choice to love or to wander down paths that lead to destruction and death.

Revelations 3:20–21 states, "Look! I am standing at the door and knocking. If anyone listens to my voice and opens the door, I will come into him and eat with him, and he will eat with me. I will give a place to sit with me on my throne to the one who overcomes, just as I have overcome and have sat down with my Father on his throne."

Nothing is unnoticed. Everything is counted. There is no religion within the ARISE Academy and no need for it. We are one family. Masters of our own life and students of Spirit who walk in compassion side by side.

I was overjoyed to have conversations like this with Sally, and she was coming to the same conclusions that I was. A beautiful friendship and sisterhood was blossoming. Sally had been spending time listening to near death experiences and studying the quantum field. She understood what I was sharing, and the keys were opening doors that she had long forgotten about but recognized in her soul. She was healing and transforming as well.

One night, I invited her to dinner. I had just set up a room in my little house that I would use for one-on-one sessions with clients, and I was excited to share it with her. Upon returning from the mini market up the road with some wine and dessert, I noticed a tiny kitten next to a trashcan. My heart dropped. What was it doing there?

Its blue eyes were wide as I came closer, but it didn't try to get away. The kitten seemed calm, so I picked it up and cradled it in my arms. It could not have been older than eight or nine weeks. I could tell that something was wrong with its legs—hence why it didn't try to run from me. A few neighbors passing by observed as I asked them if they knew who this little cat belonged to, but no one did. No matter. It was mine now.

I couldn't bring it into the house because of my dogs and its fragility. It was so delicate, and I was careful to not inflict any more distress. I placed it in my car and went inside to get it a cushion, a blanket, and some milk. Tucked warmly and lovingly in its new bed, the little kitty relaxed, just quietly laying there in comfort and taking it all in.

Sally arrived and I shared about our little visitor. "What are you going to do with it?" she asked.

"I don't know," I admitted. I'd called the association for lost animals in our neighborhood, and they said if it was alive in the morning, I should take it to the vet and then I could bring it to them should I choose to not keep it. "I am just loving it as that is the only thing I can do for it right now."

We enjoyed our dinner. I was excited to show her the sanctuary. As she stepped into the room she immediately was met by the energy. She sat and wept with a deep release, showing me that I had created a space filled with the divine energy without me doing anything. As we sat in the presence, she asked me if there were any masters around us. I smiled. "Always," I said confidently, as it is only a question of

Chapter Eight — Consciousness: The Cornerstone of Creation

tapping in. We started to tune in and to my left I saw the bright and beautiful presence of a master come into my awareness.

It was Anubis, the keeper of the door of death. An authority and warrior power that made me shudder in its magnificence and eternally loving presence. Deep reverence fell in the room as he stood and smiled at me. He had come to fetch the kitten. I knew that the little cat was passing in that exact moment and tears flooded my eyes.

Anubis lovingly communicated telepathically for me not to weep for this little one. It was returning home now. He was pleased and grateful that I had picked the kitten up. He shared his delight as a warm hug, informing me that due to my action, this little one had known the power, comfort, and pleasure of love. My heart was still broken. Surely every living creature deserves more than just two hours of love. Every being deserves so much more that they are getting out of this life.

Yes, he agreed.

Instantly, I started to feel a surge of power that I had never experienced before. A profound deep mystery and mixture of frustration and anguish mixed with a potent liberation of strength that filled my body. My arms and legs were changing, and I felt like I was taking the shape of a tiger. This was new and unfamiliar, but natural at the same time. I got bigger and bigger, with a strength that cannot be described. I saw myself hanging in space looking at the Earth as a whole planet. Tapping into my essence. It was the most incredible, ecstatic, orgasmic feeling I had ever experienced. My primal force was activating.

As I hung in space, I saw a magnificent golden lion walking regally toward me. I felt my newfound power surge through my body. Roar! I greeted Him and immediately, without hesitation and the deepest reverence, I bowed, acknowledging my King. He was pleased and I felt His love fill my heart expelling all dismay and darkness. I raised my head again, our eyes locking. The earth between us. The masculine Christ and the feminine. Inner union in a way I had never even imagined. It was my move. I felt it through his eyes.

Guided by Spirit, I lifted my right paw, claws out, and tore the veil. "Masculine!" I roared. "Arise. Take your place. Remember your honor, your power, and your promise. Respect and reverence all life. Love your woman, your children, and your animals, and restore peace." Likewise, I lifted my left paw and again tore the veil the shreds. "Feminine! Arise. Take your place, magnificent one. Remember your power, beauty, and gifts. You are the keeper of life and allow no one to dominate you."

I then saw the light coming down from the cosmos, surrounding and filling the earth. There was nowhere to hide from it.

"Leaders." My focus shifted. "He came to you as a lamb. He showed compassion, patience, gentleness, and kindness. You didn't recognize Him. You didn't choose to know Him. Now He returns as a lion and you are held to account for what you have done."

It was tremendous. My body shook as the immense transmission filled every cell. It felt like each of my cells rippled with the consciousness of a person, all the humanity of Earth. Some were terrified because they knew the harm, destruction, and war they had created. Most people rejoiced, relieved as justice was restored. I looked into the lion's eyes and felt His deep appreciation and honoring, I bowed again. The ceremony was complete, and I felt myself shrink back into my everyday awareness and natural form.

It was the most exhilarating and exponentially divine experience I had ever had. It was an activation of my legacy. Sally observed the entire event and sat in awe and reverence. This entire experience was

Chapter Eight — Consciousness: The Cornerstone of Creation

shared with me to represent the collective need to understand the body of Christ. Each of us is an entire body that has the potential to do great good and great harm, no matter how insignificant we may believe ourselves to be. That is the only illusion to overcome. This is power we represent each in our own consciousness.

"What did you see?" I asked her, curious as to her perspective of what had just happened.

"Wow, wow, wow," she said. She had never felt such majesty or such power before in her life either. "I'm so grateful that I know you," she continued. "I could see your body shifting and the gestures of the tiger. I could feel your size. Physically though, only your eyes changed."

"My eyes?"

"Oh yes. From the moment when you looked up and acknowledge the Lion, your eyes were completely black." She too had recognized Christ in her spirit.

My pupils had dilated so large that not only did they cover my iris, but also the white part. The pupils of our eyes change in order to control how much light enters the eye. In bright light the pupils get small and in the dark they grow wider so to take in more information. This said to me that I had been willing to see and had been shown the darkest dark. In that dark, I had been shown the true light of our authority and the flimsy pretense of power that creates chaos in our world.

We went out to see the little cat, and with gloves gently placed the limp body in a plastic bag. I asked Spirit what I should do with it. I was instructed to return it to the Mother and bury the body. The next day, Sally and I went to one of my favorite peaceful spots in nature, on the lake and under a tree. We returned its little body back to the arms of Mother Earth.

It was in that tender moment that Spirit whispered ever so gently, "You have wanted to know your gift."

"Yes, Spirit," I replied. "More than anything. If I understand my gift, I will know what to do." Or so I thought. I could feel Spirit sigh.

"Did you see the cat when it was alive?"

Yes.

"Did you see the cat when it was dead?"

Yes

"Do you see the difference."

Oh, yes. Clear as day.

"That is your gift! You bring life. You are life. You discern. That is your gift."

This is the clearest way I can explain what Consciousness is. It is our power. It is our life, and it is our birth right. Perspective and the light we allow, together with the free will to choose our attitude to react.

It is revelation of the very way we co-create within our reality.

Recall, dear one, at the beginning of this book, I said that you may not think that your life is the very gift itself. Yet it truly is. The light is life. The power is within us in every single cell and atom of our being. Death or separation only occurs when the light is turned off, and we are left with the vessel that once held it. I knew the little kitty was with Anubis, and just like that I understood. We are already whole and complete as the light. What we choose to align with, what we choose to create and do with our time and space, is the ultimate gift.

The process I was being shown, and now share with you, is the reclaiming of that power. The ability to stand righteously with our Christed essence that longs to restore balance, order, consciousness, and justice for self and the whole.

So, what do we choose? Life or death? Love or fear?

THE CURSE AND THE CURE

You may be wondering, as I did: if there is so much power in consciousness, why don't we see more of this in the world? Why is it so important to invest time and space in our own multidimensional mastery? Systematically, in the world we are living in, within the third dimension, we have been talked out of our power. Why? Because when you are in your full power, you are not able to be lied to, controlled, or manipulated. No one can take your money. No one can tell you what to do with your body. No one can steal your energy. And the lower matrix does not survive without feeding off us. The lower matrix is the organized fear programming and conditioning that has caused us to fear our very own light and power.

It was through this and other moments of revelation and sacred memory that Spirit shared what we need to heal as a collection of individuals.

Without entering into any paradigm of belief or dogma, there are three parts to heal. The same parts I was shown when I was in the consciousness of my tiger essence. The trinity or triune being we were designed to be. The masculine, the feminine, and the snake (or light) need to be redeemed in each of us.

I understand that the work Jeshua completed in human form was the restoration and redemption back into Everyday Eden. The original design and template for our planet and species. The message, pristine and powerful, was then taken and distorted for profit made by dominating others.

I had always known this somehow deep within, but had heard

from everyone that this is the way the world works. Perhaps it is the way it *has* worked, since the fall and until now. And, as we have been programmed that we are fallen, we have accepted this curse. In truth, the solution was given 2,000 years ago when Jeshua declared on the cross that it was finished.

It is finished when we decided to stop accommodating or complying with a game where we have been set up to lose. It is ironic that I needed to lose everything to realize that I can never lose what is most important. It is within each and every one of us. Our natural divinity was paid for, fair and square, and by grace we can receive it. This is our invitation to ARISE.

(YEAR OF THE DRAGON INITIATION)

Holy Ground. Holy Ground. Holy Ground.
Holy, Holy Ground.
Freedom to breathe.
Freedom to fly.
My wings. My wings, Father.
The wings are returning so that the kids—
so the kids, no no no no—
the Sons. the Daughters
can fly again!

For eons, you have been sworn to silence,
and now the Mother calls.
Now the Mother calls you into freedom
in service for liberation,
for their blindness.
Open the veil, beloved.
Open the veil, beloved,
and step into pure activation and deliverance.
Holy, Holy, Holy Heart (Wholeness)!

No more. No more. No more. No more.
This love. This power. This light is for you and for me.
You don't have to pay to be here. No more.
Receive your birthright. Sovereignty, beloved.
Queendom. The true feminine in her glory.
In her power. In her service. Returns. To be adored.

The Masculine. Oh brother, there are going to be
some re-negotiations, my friend.
There has to be some re-negotiations here, beloved.
Do not run from me. I love you
But do not use me. Do not test me.
Do not push me. Do not anger me.
Enough. Enough games.
My power is to honor you, beloved.
Just love me. Just hold me. Just see me.
I am tired of these games you play with my holiness (wholeness).
No more. No more, beloved.

Unity. Harmony. Oneness. Returns.
The power of the serpent unleashed
Holy Ground. Holy Ground. We are Holy Ground.
Sisters. Women. Side by side.
Mother. Daughter. Side by side.
Priestess. Peasant. Side by side
on Holy Ground. Mother, may it be so.
Unity with women.
Unity with men.
Unity for the sons and the daughters
of the most high living God.

(Year of the Dragon Initiation)

Into the ground, deep. deep. deep.
Seeds have been planted here.
I step in. Into the roots of the seed.
Thank you! Stepping into the roots of this place
in service to Gaia. Feel these roots. A network of light.
Roots of light go deep, laid by the ancestors.
A network laid in the etheric. Feel these roots.
The druids. The wizards. The witches. The Magi. Thank you.
Roots of light go down deep into the Earth.
In the core, pulling up the fire from the core.
The true light of the Earth.
Planetary Consciousness.
Up through the earth.

The Mother says, "I hear you my daughter."
Tired of the fires, I have burnt. I have burnt.
I have burnt. I have burnt.
I am purified. I have burnt. I have burnt.
"I know," says the Mother.
Every step, I have seen.
Every step, I have carried you.
Now, I bring you the purest of living waters.
Overflow, overflow. Ease. Life. Abundance.
Mentally. Emotionally. Physically. Energetically.
Drink. Drink. Drink. Drink, my love,
from the waters of life.

Thank you, Father. Thank you, Mother.
I love you. I love you. I love you.

Thank you, Jeshua. Thank you, Mary Magdalene.
Michael. Gabriel. Rafael. Uriel.
Holy Ground. And so it is.
Abba, Mother and Father.

CHAPTER NINE
Congruence: Everything Is Momentum

It is one thing to know something intellectually. It is quite another to apply and walk it on a daily basis. Navigating the paradox of our infinite potential and the manifest reality we are living in is challenging. How do we effectively transform something when the circumstance is seemingly so fixed and solid? That is why there is an Essential Ecosystem process, and this is where the art of congruence comes into our journey of wholeness.

Congruence is the fixed focus and daily momentum we apply as we dissolve and alchemize the paradoxes that we have been conditioned and programmed to believe in. These subconscious and unconscious belief systems are invisible to the naked eye and hidden from view. I had no clue that this was the one thing that was stopping me from truly advancing in my calling.

To anchor this vast wisdom within our essence, into our everyday reality, requires the mastery of our focus. This is the only single thing that we have absolute control over. This is where we take this understanding and integrate it step by step into everyday application.

I have come to understand multidimensional mastery as the ability to be in a physical situation while also present and connected to the higher perspective. The mastery of receiving and perceiving all information being presented, allowing us to feel it and yet not being swept away by fear nor reaction. A conscious choice of creation is our access point to enlightenment.

Within my deep, personal, and all-encompassing quest, I noticed that transformation is always twofold. It is about discovering the new and unknown, learning the new lessons and manifesting the change we desire. Just as much, it is about uncovering the consistent timeless sameness. The unchanging, permanent, and natural part of ourselves that we can place our feet upon creates the necessary stability we need. It is a journey of ascension to know the higher as well as a journey of embodiment to establish the lower in alignment.

As we navigate the matrix of time and space now, we understand that every moment is new and unique, and all change and new decisions are possible. We are always influenced by what has been and what we project and expect will happen next.

Through this work, I have come to understand that the shift we are navigating right now has to do with a fundamental and crucial choice point we are making as humanity. This seems like a slight shift, but it is truly massive and affects the way we understand all relationships around us.

How do we give and receive?

A new way is needed. One of peace, abundance, and plenty. Reciprocal relationships where give-and-take is balanced, fair, and just. For too long we have been separated into those who have and those who do not. Those who seem chosen and those who appear to not count. We are being asked to go higher, and I have been shown that we are moving from this limited paradigm into which we have been indoctrinated and into to an abundant and limitless paradigm of give and receive.

Within evolutionary theory, we are told consistently that life is a jungle and it's survival of the fittest. That was the hamster wheel I had been on for all of my adult life. Placed into competition and comparison, which Jeshua called foolishness. As we truly evolve, we find that the "fittest" is found in collaboration, not separation. The individual within the collective. How do we compete when we are unique—and why would we even try? Who are we without support? We all need each other.

Within this evolution, we have a new option of freedom and true expression. This is where we personally own our unique genius, our authentic brand of special ability that only we can do. It cannot be stolen, copied, or replaced. And I believe it is the most important new leadership development in a time where we are constantly bombarded with the narrative that a robot can do everything one hundred times better than a human. This is a psyop (a military term for psychological operations) of the most malignant kind.

As the creator of artificial intelligence, human intelligence is the *only* intelligence that can create something unique and original. That makes it superior by definition. Artificial intelligence, however helpful, will only ever be able to replicate and recreate what has already been input. Humankind is the only species known to us at this time that can create from nothing.

Inspiration: the art of being in Spirit, of being connected to the divine and untainted flow of creation that we are cultivating. Consciousness in motion and momentum. By developing and leveraging our unique gifts, we can show and up and create a new space in the world that contributes and generates unique value. This requires a new momentum in our everyday lives. Not a never-ending war against flesh and blood, but a reclamation of the innate and eternal value that we are in sacred service to others around us. To enter this, we only need to trade the paradigm of survival for the understanding of surrender.

As an empowered, Christed person, you serve the world the

greatest by literally being you. The only thing that matters is discovering the real you day by day. Allowing yourself to be that person takes daily, constant focus. If this one thing is your focus, everything around you will flourish. Just allow yourself to explore and express new situations, ideas, and sensations. This is the great evolution and adventure. Congruence might become habitual or religious, yet I have seen our true divine nature is endless and creative. We are multidimensional co-creators. The sky is the limit.

BECOMING THE TEACHER

In September 2024, we were starting the fourth year of the ARISE Collective and we were growing. Valerie, Carole (a soul sister in Switzerland), and Sally were my constant and steadfast companions on the journey. Now we welcomed two pioneer students from the United Kingdom: Varvara, an artist and schoolteacher, and Angela, a devoted wife, mother, and avid musician. Both were initiated in the three-month journey to establish their own unique Essential Ecosystem and would continue to receive support to ground and integrate the transformation for the coming nine months.

It was incredible to watch how they used meditations, teachings, and videos. Valerie's scan helped the participants track their changes and focus on what was needed. I knew I had created the experience I most wanted to serve people with. The great part was that most was done in the time and pace of the student and on the ARISE app, which Valerie had supported me to create. It was a joy to serve and most importantly, it was effortless, only costing me an extra one-on-one session per student per month.

The results were mind blowing. In the words of the other pioneer, Angela, as a result of the three-month Essential Ecosystem

Experience: "I have learned so much from being with the ARISE Academy through all the teachings and meditations. I have benefited from the calm and supportive and safe environment that you foster. I've loved digging deeper and growing in my own awareness. This has helped me realize the reasons why my health has been deteriorating over the last few years. I had been over giving to others and not prioritizing me for as long as I can remember. Through this process I have learned to relax (which I never thought was possible as I'm always so busy). I have learned to hold space for myself and change my priorities. This process has been really enlightening. It has helped me remember who I am and supported me to make changes in my life which means that I now have a much better balance. I am gaining strength and am losing weight which now means that when I choose to help others I am not giving all my energy away. I no longer serve from an empty cup. I make sure that I take time out to meditate and this helps set me up for the day ahead. I now feel like I am winning. At this moment I am happy to say that I am over a stone lighter, have stopped taking multiple painkillers and I have greater peace. I'll be forever grateful to you, Lizete for such a gift.

Valerie had been my main financial supporter for the last three years. She understood what I was building and wanted to invest in the Academy. She had been following another mentor she greatly appreciated, Peter Sage, who was originally from the United Kingdom and currently living in Tenerife. He was holding his last Millionaire Business School event, and she was adamant that we should go together.

I didn't have the finances at the time. Not even to buy my flight. As the days grew closer, with the training and the accommodation fully paid for, she took another step in faith and bought my ticket. I was amazed and a bit resistant—something I was working on healing. I could hardly believe that someone wanted to pay all this money just to have me in the room with her to learn what she believed I needed to learn. But she believed in the ARISE Academy just as much as I did and wanted to launch it to the wider public.

I accepted her gift with trembling hands and watched as everything started to fall into place. At the airport, I was nervous. This was my first time outside of my cocoon of the Alentejo in over two years and my first flight since my return from Costa Rica in 2021.

I tuned into and asked Spirit, "Is this real? Can I really be a millionaire?"

The answer came immediately. "You will never need to be frustrated again."

I was shocked at the response, knowing I could never have made that up. Frustration had been my constant companion.

"You can have whatever you decide, as long as you don't forget the purity." Instantly I knew that this purity was the golden rule I had been shown over and over. *Never place yourself above. Never place yourself below. Side by side. Allow it to flow.*

When I arrived, I met up with Valerie. She reeled as she saw me, delighted to see me in person and in utter shock at my physical presence. "You are stunning, my love. You look like a model." I don't really look like a model, but it was lovely to hear, and what she meant was my body had transformed into its natural state. My body was indeed very different from when we had last had a hug in person at Enxara in May of 2022. We got into the taxi and made our way to the venue.

The luxury and the beauty of this hotel was breathtaking. It boasted large courtyards with flowing fountains and filled with beautifully decorated furnishings; everything needed for a relaxed, comfortable, and inspired visit. We were right at home. We were going to spend a week here together—four of those days training with Peter Sage and his academy, learning all the strategies needed to take my ideas and content and turn it into a millionaire enterprise.

The first morning of the training was for Elite members who had completed the six-month program, as Valerie had done. We went into the very large event training room. As we stood there with over one hundred and fifty students from around the world, Peter came on stage and was welcomed with gratitude and adoration. I could tell the difference he had made in the lives of these people, and it filled my heart. Peter had the presence of a leader. Fearless, confident, and friendly all rolled into one. A confident man in committed service is sexy! Period.

I stepped out for a moment to go to the bathroom and when I returned, the participants were in small groups, sharing with each other what had brought them to this very moment in the room. I stayed on the outskirts, looking on, feeling into the space, and watching the energy shift from a group of strangers to a cohesive collective of people all sharing their stories and finding the commonalities that unified them all.

As I watched, Spirit asked me, "Do you want this? This life of teaching others?"

Yes, it was what I wanted my whole life. To sing and teach on a stage like this. To work and be present in a room full of students just like this. There is nothing I wanted more. "Yes Spirit. This is what I want." The true teaching had begun.

Peter stepped off the stage and made his way around the room, eventually coming over to me. "Is everything okay, Lizete?" he asked.

I immediately felt his energy field as he came closer. "Everything is perfect, Peter, thank you. I am observing the field," I offered as an explanation, sensing he would understand. He nodded. "I want to thank you for everything you are doing in the name of global consciousness," I continued, the words steady and sure.

He looked at me, and I felt that he could see me. Really see me. And to my delight he was intrigued, not afraid nor intimidated.

For so long I had been surrounded by men who felt threatened because I can see through the story and physical narrative into the essence. This man had nothing to hide. I liked that and understood I was safe.

The next day, the Millionaire Business School began, with about four hundred and fifty more participants than the day before. The teaching, the tools, and the training were top notch. Ideas flowed and clarity about how to piece together the different areas of the ARISE Academy came into clear focus. I truly had built everything I needed over the last two and a half years, and excitedly, I shared the structure I was creating with Valerie. She was delighted. This was what she knew would happen when I was exposed to the genius that Peter uniquely carried.

On the third day of training, I got the breakthrough I had come to Tenerife to receive. It was visceral transformation. An important question had come up. Peter was asking the group why we wanted to be millionaires, "Why do you want the money?"

A woman on a table to my right raised her hand. "With that kind of money, I could give it to the poor to end all the suffering." I recognized myself immediately in her answer, and I also knew it was not "right" but didn't know why.

Immediately the woman right in front of me muttered, "Give your money away? Girl, don't be crazy. People will just take it and then throw you away." I recognized myself in this too. I had been cast aside by people the minute they had what they wanted. I was not going to be used anymore. This was exactly my millionaire money paradox.

This was the moment, the question I had been grappling with

Chapter Nine — Congruence: Everything Is Momentum

when it came to manifesting my physical abundance and worth. I looked up to Peter curious as to what he would say to this. He had not heard the lady to my left, and yet it mattered not.

"You don't need to give your money away to save others. You don't have to save anyone when you can simply inspire them to create their own wealth and find their own way to have the abundance they deserve."

Bam! His words landed and I felt a visceral explosion in my solar plexus. A big bang happening within the inside of my universe. *What? I don't have to save anyone? I don't have to be used by anyone?* Shivers coursed through my system like I had been hit by lightning. I get to live my life as an inspiration for someone else, in service to my authentic gifts? Wow. They will make their own money, and I get to keep mine.

It was the key I had waited for my whole life.

Your keys will be unique to you. This was such a powerful moment for three specific reasons, which are the lessons we all need to learn and receive from one another:

- I had respect and appreciation for Peter, an individual who was stating his truth and was speaking from experience as a manifested authority on the topic. He had inspired many to make their own money and embodied generosity, sharing his stage and introducing us to some of them. (Masculine, sovereign, and active.)

- I was willing to admit to myself I didn't have the answer. I was looking for the answer and willing to listen and receive his advice. I had already reached the end of my ego on this, and this is when we can truly receive. (Feminine, sacred service and passive.)

- What Peter shared was in alignment with the authority I had in my life, which was Jeshua. It truly didn't matter if I became a millionaire if all it meant was that I'd have relationships I couldn't trust. Nor did I have any need to be the go-to person to help people out of financial struggle. (Natural divinity, security, and manifest balance.)

We are each equipped to create the reality we desire and are—dare I say—destined for. Each of us has, thus far, one choice at a time. If we don't like it, we can transform it and are invited to do so. Each of us created in the image of God. Whole in ourselves. Jeshua has already come to save by establishing the bridge between the third dimension and the multidimensional reality available to all who will believe and receive.

I am here to simply be Lizete. I was created to inspire. I, like you, was born to be free.

This is the power of teaching and learning from others. Peter's role serves as an example. Our teachers share reassuring experiences, tools, and keys that we have not yet received. This sparks the energetic revelation that frees us from the environment that seeks to control us or dumb us down.

This has become my clear understanding of the role we each play in the lives of others as we continue to develop and evolve our consciousness. We are all teaching and modeling different possibilities for each other. We no need longer someone to tell us the whole truth and nothing but the truth. A good teacher demonstrates their unique truth in every second. If we are wise, we know what we know and we are aware that we don't know many other wonderful and fantastic things. We can be teachers and students in each moment while we all navigate the unknowable together. This is our possibility to create the future.

The new leaders and teachers of this time will lead by example, and that happens through practicing congruence on an everyday basis with each powerful step and decision we make. Taking time to heal is just as important as taking time to create. The entire journey of Alignment through the lens of consciousness is to be congruent with our inner soul and create a safe space to explore the legacy we are here to create.

THE LIES OF THE LOWER MATRIX

We have been hijacked by a lower matrix of consciousness that I have been studying my whole life. As I was unraveling layers of revelation, I was also being shown layers of deception. These lies have been embedded deeply in our systems as we unconsciously accept the authority of others to dictate our reality.

There are specifically five critical deceptions I will cover here that shifted my congruence and the directional focus of my momentum in beautiful and incredible ways. As we dispel and examine these deceptions, notice what it has cost to accept these illusions and remember that you can always change your mind. We are all free to choose. So, let us choose.

To deepen our understanding of the impact of these deceptions I will link them to the dimensions and to our bodies so we can detect for ourselves the impact of these cultural spoon-fed beliefs.

Lie #1: You Can't Handle the Truth
(AIR/FIRST DIMENSION/MENTAL BODY)

This iconic phrase is from the film *A Few Good Men*, but the moment has lasted because it contains a universal feeling. When children question why certain difficult things are the way they are, they are often met with vague answers. Parents don't want to explain why some people are living on the streets. They want to shield their child from the fact of death. But children know instinctively they are not getting the full story, and they become fearful.

INDEPENDENCE/ CONGRUENCE
The Lies of the Lower Matrix

AIR ELEMENT

LIE: "You can't handle the truth."
TRUTH: The truth will set you free.

WATER ELEMENT

LIE: "Life is an illusion."
TRUTH: Life is the only thing that is real.

SPACE ELEMENT

LIE: "There can only be one."
TRUTH: We are all "The One."

FIRE ELEMENT

LIE: "Money makes the world go round."
TRUTH: We can master giving and receiving in equal measure.

EARTH ELEMENT

LIE: "Sex work was the first profession."
TRUTH: Manipulation makes whole men and women doubt their wholeness.

Chapter Nine — Congruence: Everything Is Momentum

We have been conditioned to be afraid of the truth. As if when we do hear the truth, it will be so shocking and awful that we realize it is best to leave it to the people that understand those things.

Jeshua said, "You shall know the truth and the truth, will set you free." It has been proven in my experience repeatedly that while some truth is painful, once we know it, we have the tools to actually deal with whatever situation presents itself. It is a sovereign choice to desire to know truth.

I remember sitting at the lake that bordered my town flat in the Netherlands. This was the place I had come when I was just twenty-one, in love, full of hopes and dreams, and ready to start married life. A successful but exhausting executive career and fifteen years later, I sat there frustrated and desperate, tears streaming down my face. I had just realized my husband had been unfaithful for at least seven years of our marriage, while I had shriveled and starved in my inner sanctuary for most of my late twenties and early thirties. He was a good man but couldn't be faithful. I had known it deep inside but not acknowledged it until this moment, when it slapped me in the face and could no longer be ignored. I was no longer his type. It was in that moment I made a heart-filled and complete decision that radically changed my life. And it was the best one I could have made.

Instead of "I can't handle the truth," we can tell ourselves, "I want to know the truth, I can handle the truth just fine. The truth sets me free."

I don't want fairytale stories. I am done with illusion and lies. That was the beginning of my promise to never lie to myself. While we are eternal, I still don't like to waste time in illusions and lies. This is a key to advanced evolutionary growth in multidimensional mastery.

I knew something was wrong. I thought I needed to find out what was wrong. In truth, I only needed to know that my needs mattered, and they were not being met. That has been the journey. Now, it is only possible for people to lie to me when I have a vested ego interest in what they are saying. A promise that I hope for, a need, or a codependency. Instead, I have learned to focus on truth and the truth always manifests into matter.

Everything I have discovered about the human body—the emotional power of our waters, the music, and the multidimensional gifts—have been revealed because I am willing to see and feel and know the truth being shown. When someone shows me that they don't care, I believe them. When someone does care, I can tell the difference. To know the truth, we only need to be willing to have this courage. The result of knowing the truth that others try to hide is that we separate, and things end as we know them. That was the case for me and my marriage, but the good news is that we are never alone. When we navigate and choose to know truth, we uncover that our soul, our higher self is always with us.

Life is An Illusion
(WATER/SECOND DIMENSION/EMOTIONAL BODY)

A common phrase I've heard from spiritual teachers is "Life is an illusion."

I know in every cell in my being that this is false. Life is the *only* thing that is real. Another version of this dogma is, "Life is like a video game." I understand the concept, and while I have mastered focus, what we focus on grows because it has our conscious attention. That doesn't mean that life is still not happening regardless.

Often I hear, "If a tree falls in the forest and I didn't see it, did it really fall?" Yes. Of course it fell. I am not the god of the universe, so if it fell, it fell. Whether or not I experience the tree falling, my awareness did not make it happen. Life is happening with or without me—or you. I assure you.

The reason this confusion is so important is because it locks us into a comfort zone of superiority that sooner or later is going to kick our butts. It also stifles our heart and emotions. It makes us afraid to feel, but to feel is our superpower. The truth is, there is an illusion, but it is not life. The illusion is *death*, my friend.

Death certainly felt real the day I stood in front of my dad's coffin on December 29, 2013. My hands touched the box that held the body of the one I had most loved and respected. My provider, my protector, my principal council. My hero was dead. My heart broke in a way I thought would never be repaired. I leaned over to give him a final kiss, and my lips touched ice cold flesh that made me recoil. My father was no longer there. He had gone.

Death felt so real, and I could not distract myself from it or run away. But as I allowed it, I found that death was there to support me to awaken deeper. Through my multidimensional mastery of navigating through time and speaking with the masters, I came to understand that death is not an actual ending of life. It is only an end to this particular incarnation. We are separated from the body as the soul returns to its original state and beingness before moving onward to the next life.

In 2024, my mom called me one morning. "There was someone here last night!" she said.

"Do you have any idea of who?" I asked.

"Not sure, but I wasn't afraid. I was sleeping when I heard glass break in the kitchen. I woke up when I heard it, but it didn't feel threatening. Only in the morning I saw it was a decorative plate fixed to the wall. It didn't fall by itself. The frame and nail were still in the wall."

I asked her if she would like to enter the field with me. She did. I picked up my crystalline bowl and started singing. Within a minute her tears started flowing. "I know who it was."

My father.

"He is upset because they are moving his bones out of the grave and putting them in a box. He is scared that we won't be able to find him."

Guided by Spirit, I instinctively went higher and felt catapulted in speeds that I had never experienced before. I was zooming and zooming around the universe, looking and looking. I had never done this before and had never known anyone to do it, but it was the most exhilarating and powerful feeling. Soon I saw what I was searching for. It looked like a nebula. A cloud of gray that held a vast group of people. As I stood there, hanging in space, I spotted my father and locked onto him with my gaze. I lifted him up and out of the nebula and drew him toward myself. I distinctly noticed my royal presence, though this had no emotion and was just fact.

I looked at him standing in front of me and asked seriously, "Do you see me now, dear one?"

"Yes," he whispered. I could sense his reverence and awe.

"Do you think that there is anywhere in this universe that you could go where my love would not find you?" My body shook with the power and conviction of my words that sounded thunderous.

He shook his head.

"Now you have a choice."

Without a second of hesitation, his being embraced me and I felt the full impact of all the emotion I had held in my field and being. It was him. There was no mistake. His embrace, his presence, his soul signature. The tears that I thought had dried up years before burst through like a raging dam opening its portals. Daddy. He stepped into my field on my left side, just behind my shoulder and took his place.

It was the last time I have ever missed my father. I now feel him with me all the time in a comfortable way. I have evolved to learn how to love and listen to him while still being sovereign and doing what I am here to do. Our relationship of approval and authority had changed, but my love for him is eternal, as is his for me.

This is why death is the illusion. Life is the truth and when we pass on, we continue to live out the consequences and lessons in a different from. Our consciousness does not end. All souls that have ever been or lived are still present in some sort of frequency of consciousness.

Lie #3: Sex Work Was the First Profession
(EARTH/THIRD DIMENSION/PHYSICAL BODY)

I can't remember the first time I ever heard this lie. There is no evidence, no reason to believe it is true, yet it is a common belief.

When we reduce people, especially women, to sex workers, it creates separation and conflict. Yet sex work comes in many forms. Society teaches women to be threatened by the beauty of others, and we are encouraged from a young age to take the confirmation of beauty from other people as a badge of honor, belonging, and value.

I believe the sole reason for this fabrication is to give permission to men to enjoy the pleasures of having a wife they esteem who will stand with them in public and keep their home for them. At the same time, these good wives are starved out of the expression of their true sexual nature. They have others for that. Although times are changing and have changed, allowing for sex work to be a valid profession, I am highlighting a polarized reality that we are healing from, as sex work as degradation was the norm for thousands of years. The feminine energy was not valued in her singularity. As we discover more and more clearly that, no matter the body we inhabit, we will always have masculine and feminine, we understand that the balance within us as a whole human being is the key to creating partnerships and relationships of honor and respect.

I love all women. I have come to understand the perspective and the conditions that drive many women to sex work. I totally understand circumstances—not to mention how many are in this position by force or as a form of slavery. I also love all men. But what they don't seem to realize is that every woman is a portal, or a well. When you visit with a woman, you are literally tapping into her waters and drinking from her. I find it hilarious that we have spent lifetimes of crusades looking for the one cup that Jeshua drank from, as if that will give us eternal life. It is absolutely ridiculous from any perspective. An excuse appearing spiritual to pillage, steal, kill, and destroy. In a quest to find a cup.

It is not a cup that gives you eternal life, dear one—not even one drunk from by the greatest master. It is when you honor and drink from a whole woman that you will find strength. This lie from the pit of hell has completely eroded our creation energy. I have always been a sexual woman, and yet it seems to be the one thing that is consistently manipulated inside of the matrix. Who we give ourselves to sexually is a spiritual contract. So, during this time of isolation and consciously-chosen celibacy, I started cultivating my own sovereign sexual energy into my creations.

Everyone who wants to should be making love. I am all for intimacy and sovereignty over our own bodies. In truth it is the most beautiful natural and orgasmic thing. That is why I put so much effort into trying to save my relationships. When Spirit told me not to sell myself anymore, I looked at myself for the first time, honestly asking where had I prostituted myself. Had I sold myself? I had, every time that I settled for less than the reciprocal loving energy exchange that matches my true worth.

The first real occupation of anyone who studies multidimensional mastery is that our one and only occupation is to be whole. The ARISE Academy and this book offer the truth that a woman can have it all if she has support in finding her unique multidimensional gift. We can change the world by empowering all women to make their living by adding the value only they uniquely can deliver. Each must make a living, but we are told we need to work to make a living. We are finding another way by tapping into the innate and invaluable resource we are to create our own abundance, through turning our lead into gold, our love into our power.

Lie #4: Money Makes the World Go Round
(FIRE/FOURTH DIMENSION/ENERGETIC BODY)

This is a saying we have repeated until it almost seems real. Yet it is not. Money certainly does not make the world go round. People circulate money by the choices they make. Each transaction is a choice of investment and trust that they are getting what they paid for.

This lie has been ingrained to disempower you by defining your worth based on external circumstances. Between 2013 and 2018, I received between €3,500 and €4,500 a day as my teaching fee for specific clients, and up to €18,500 euros for three-day executive team retreats. Does that mean I am less valuable right now as I write this book with hardly any money coming in? Money defines nothing about our worth! We as humanity make the world go round.

This lie creates the illusion of power that the lower matrix governs itself by. The one who gives or cuts off funding is seen as the more powerful person. But that money often is not even theirs. In the case of government, it actually belongs to each individual within the nation. At best, they are trusted stewards of this wealth. The true wealth is you and me.

It was worth losing every person and every cent from that time in my life to find the treasure I have uncovered within this work. To discover the infinite health my body is generating using sound and light within my cells. Just by caring for myself—the one thing I didn't have time to do when I was working to make money. It's a little crazy-making, isn't it?

Each and every soul of humanity is sacred. I work with people for free if need be, trusting I will be provided for. For those who have the gift of money to give me, it does not buy them my knowledge or pay for my time to be with them. It is the exchange and investment in their own evolution as they choose me to guide them and benefit from the unique vibration and capacity I've developed.

I can openly and willingly receive money when it's backed up by free will and paid to honor who I am and what I give. But money will never define me again. This is why, when truly wealthy people lose everything they have, they simply make it back: they know they are the real wealth, and they have surrounded themselves with people who also perceive them to be of value. Others who have merely inherited money could go as far as suicide upon losing it—they feel it defines their whole worth, that they are nothing without it. This is how strongly we have identified with money.

We are the commodity in a world trying to convince us that we need something outside of us. When you decide you are not for sale, the game changes. You have set yourself free to discover your true spiritual and infinite inheritance given to you through your lineage, in your DNA and encoded in your very being. It is a journey we take one step at a time.

Lie #5: There Can Be Only One
(SPACE/FIFTH DIMENSION/SOUL BODY)

This last lie was trickiest to spot, but it hit home with a bang. We generally feel safe with what is familiar. With new or very different things, we are either intrigued and curious or judge them and run away terrified.

As I was claiming my authenticity and devoting myself to my journey, I noticed that I had no tension, friction, or confusion with people who had the willingness and patience to understand me. The exchange of energies flowed easily and beautifully. As I was walking consciously without attachment, some relationships would mature and develop. I noticed a deep distinction that I had previously been unaware of. Even for those who embraced me, chaos would erupt the minute they started comparing and competing with me on some level. I would feel it. A closing of the heart. The decline in vulnerable sharing. A coldness that seemed to have no reason.

Then I realized it was this lie—that there could only be one—unconsciously working on us in the shadows of our own insecurity. It is the competitive mind that says, "If that person is succeeding, there isn't any space for me to succeed. If they are shining or strong, it means I am weaker or at risk."

This retraction of emotion was something I had suffered throughout my relationship with Nathan. My survival strategy was to forgive and then keep giving generously to win him back. What I hadn't seen in this behavior was that I was completely selling myself out and would inevitably end up heartbroken. Over and over. Not because he left, but because I had given without receiving. I was always left empty-handed.

When love stops flowing effortlessly and voluntarily in a relationship, that person has ceased to be a safe space. This is the same for any kind of relationship. For example, people may feel comfortable with me on one level, but as I evolve and elevate, they may make judgments on that. The people who eventually start competing and comparing did love me— but not for me. They loved how I made them feel. They loved what I did for them. They loved what I could bring them, but their love was not real. They didn't actually love me as I truly was. To simply walk away from those relationships was a hard lesson to learn.

I stepped away from comparing and competing when I realized we cannot be anything else but ourselves. I cannot be anything but me, and to compare unique beings prohibits the exact genius the other is here to cultivate and express. Side by side in harmony means each in their own strength.

We are each the one in our own universe. We each create our own script and sing our unique song with our authentic voice. Some will love it, and some will run. The runners are the easier ones to spot. The ones who stay will still need to be shuffled through to know who is truly with us and who is hanging on our coattails because they think we are going to take them somewhere. This revelation brought me the understanding of why Jesus said, in Matthew 25:12: "But he replied, 'I tell all of you with certainty, I don't know you!'" How could unconditional love not know someone? Yet, today, I do understand this. The one was Jeshua, and He came for the whole of each of us. There is no higher or lower, just different and unique.

For us to truly receive someone else, we have to be madly and passionately in love with our own unique calling so much that we would never want to compete or compare. It only works in harmony, when each person loves and accepts the role they are here to play.

Here again we see the same pattern repeat of what Master Jeshua spoke about: "Love thy God and love each other. This is the fulfillment of the law." If we can tap into this love intelligence, empowered to fulfill our role while honoring the role of the other, we will always have full access to our natural divinity.

This is how we build communities and friendships that we can know and trust. We know who has our backs. We have a mutual benefit. We find these people by connecting with the flow of love we experience in the presence of another. If they are shut down, they are not navigating or operating in love. They are able to siphon our energy but are not giving us anything back. When you realize the imbalance that this creates in your world, you will discover that you never really lose anyone in this journey. You only let go of those who don't love you as you are.

CREATING CONGRUENCE

Congruence is to choose love consistently as you build a new momentum that creates more abundant life. There is no quick pill or shot we can take to build congruence. This is the mastery of time and space we cultivate for ourselves, and as a result, with each other. This is how we co-create. It is an experience, and that is why within the ARISE Academy we do the Essential Ecosystem Experience. Congruence is momentum built with focus on consciousness. That requires a journey. Within our three-month container, we lay the steps of the journey with meditation on the calibration of the body on a daily basis, as well as teachings to navigate your unique situation and circumstance.

INDEPENDENCE / CONGRUENCE
The Doors of the Higher Matrix

Masculine Polarity

Feminine Polarity

AIR ELEMENT

You are never alone.
You are divine and
connected to your higher self
at all times.

WATER ELEMENT

Separation is the only illusion.
All souls who have ever
been are here now.

FIRE ELEMENT

Ancient and future wisdom
and technology are
our divine inheritance, and they
are returning at this time.

EARTH ELEMENT

Everything I have been taught
to believe is up for
review and reconsideration.

CHAPTER TEN

Compassion: The Leadership of Christed Consciousness

In each language I have learned unique and irreplaceable words that I love. In Portuguese, my second language, that word is "saudade," an emotional state of longing or nostalgia for a person or thing so intense, it actually becomes a noun—an actual manifest thing that inspired a whole genre of music. During my life in the Netherlands, I learned "gunnen," a verb that means finding joy in the happiness or success of other people, celebrating them without jealousy or resentment. In English, my mother tongue, my favorite word has to be "compassion," and it is the final step of our process.

Compassion is putting everything we have walked and mastered into action. It is love in embodied form. It is the power of the divine integrated and alive in our intentions, reactions, and deeds in everyday human life. It is love on the move, in the moment.

Compassionate leadership is not new. Indeed, it is the main reason why we celebrate the greatest leaders of our time, such as Mother Teresa, Nelson Mandela, Martin Luther King, Jr., Mahatma Gandhi, and the Dalai Lama. These revered individuals all have one thing in common: in times of desolation, destruction, and suffering, they chose to use their power for peace. They chose to serve and bring people together instead of focusing on retaliation, domination, and revenge. With many different options, they did what was loving. Compassion is love in action.

The deception is that there are very few of these examples. Compassion is often portrayed as something only a few can attain and is almost, if not downright, impossible for the rest of us. That is the illusion and the devastating lie.

YOU ARE CALLED BY YOUR OWN SPIRIT

I never had ambitions to be a leader on the world stage. Not once. My dream was a simple one. I wanted to find one man. One person who I loved and who loved me in return. I wanted a place I could call home, and where I could invite others to experience for themselves what I had uncovered. I wanted to support leaders from the foundation of my peace walking side by side with the divine in the cool of the day.

I call this place Everyday Eden because the original idea of Eden still beckons us and is compassion embodied. We were created to walk in love with one another. This is the original blueprint—and we have been conditioned to believe it is Mission Impossible when in fact it is the road of least resistance and greatest ease. Love can heal the world, and love can only thrive when we make decisions in alignment with this knowing.

In our everyday reality, it becomes easier to see, sense, and know that it is the Mother who sustains, nourishes, and loves all her children, even though she has been demonized, ignored, used, and abused. It is the loving Father, often misunderstood or feared, who is galactic consciousness, ensuring in perfect order that the creation operates without fail. We are healing ourselves and restoring order, starting with ourselves. Nothing more than this that is asked of any single human. This is my vision of things—the choice I have made and the insights that reshaped my reality and my legacy leadership.

Chapter Ten — Compassion: The Leadership of Christed Consciousness

What I learned along the way is that Eden is not a pipe dream. It can be real. We have all been given free will to choose how we operate in our everyday lives. We choose our contribution in every moment. And we even get free will to tear it all down with the push of a button. This is a responsibility that is not only reserved for one office, the White House, or in a faraway land. That is the illusion. It is up to each sovereign individual that is alive on planet Earth right now. No one and nothing can do anything to you unless you accept and allow it. This feminine power is the new evolution we are cultivating now. This is the power of peace and unity that is arising. This is the value of true freedom.

A saying that supports the case of compassion and our authority to choose is: "What goes around, comes around!"

We only need to look at reality to see how this saying stands the test of time. Our planet is round. It turns every day, creating our twenty-four-hour cycle of day and night. Our seasons rotate from spring, summer, autumn, winter. Nature understands these cycles of time. All other planets in our solar system are rotating around the sun. Everything that goes around comes around.

Jeshua spoke of this. What we sow, we shall reap. Every seed we plant shall have its harvest. Every action will have its equal and opposite reaction. The scientific law of cause and effect operates in our third dimension of everyday consciousness. What I choose and how I act becomes this seed and in the course of time, no matter how I try to run from it, there is nowhere to go. Things will always come back.

Jeshua gave us a golden rule to navigate this reality. A compass if you will.

Luke 6:31: "Do to others as you would have them do to you."

This is the clearest way of compassion. It is a principle of

Christed Consciousness and the foundation of this entire teaching. At the beginning of our journey, I mentioned the subtle and profound insight Spirit had whispered to me. Perspective and attitude are everything. Our journey began with awareness, which is our human ability of perspective. The attitude that is recommended in any circumstance is compassion.

OVERCOMING SEPARATION WITHIN AND WITH OTHERS

I recall being in Mexico, in that beautiful multi-colored little cabin rented for me by Sky just prior to the beginning of my journey with Nathan. The four-poster bed with the wispy, white linen covering in perfect protection. The soft, clean, and untainted sanctuary where I rested my head on the pillow that first night in the jungle. I felt like a queen. I loved to be there and was so pleased I had given this gift to myself.

    I lay there in my beautiful, comfortable bed, and there didn't seem to be a more sacred, more holy, more safe place in the universe. The only person I would ever enjoy sharing this space with was Nathan. I imagined him there, with only a few days to go before we were scheduled to meet in Costa Rica. Our love story yet unwritten.

    Suddenly I could see him lying there, sleeping right next to me. His gentle breath flowed in and out. He stirred and started to wake up. He opened his eyes and looked at me. I ran my fingers in his hair, whispering, "Good morning love." He reached out and took me in his arms. His fingers tracked my face as he smiled, his adoration felt in his tender kiss. I felt the warmth of his breath, his tongue in my mouth, the passion rising quick and fiery. The aching and longing for

Chapter Ten — Compassion: The Leadership of Christed Consciousness

him filled me as I felt him getting hard and large. His desire overtook him; he pinned me under his body. His fingers found their way to the most sacred of sanctuaries. His home. His love. His completeness.

Surrendering to the passion, desiring this man above all else, I allowed myself to fall as he entered my body, filling every cell with natural ecstasy. His rhythm was that of an ocean, surging and ebbing. This divine union, this perfection was like nothing I've ever experienced. He was both tender and gentle, while sure and strong. I felt his muscles move with grace and strength as he made me his and only his. Our sacred flame burned all else away until there was nothing left of old. The atomic energy of source creation power is the only thing that remained as our passion and love consumed us in holy fire. *I have waited for you my whole life, beloved. My body has ached for you, my heart has longed for you. My soul was always convinced you were always on your way. Now I have come home to my completeness and my sacred union.*

That was the highest ambition of my life. My template of true happiness and love shared, in the sanctuary of intimacy, with my beloved. And indeed, I am grateful that I've experienced this in real life, if only for a few moments. These moments were sometimes weeks, sometimes days, sometimes glimpses, but I lived it and will always be eternally grateful.

The relationship didn't work—it imploded and self-destructed. But why? The passion and fire potential had not found its flow or balance. Now, I was learning to balance it for myself. The passion that is the fuel of all life, creation, intimacy, and internal fulfillment. That was my quest. To have it all is to have those moments in the container that is my everyday life and service. It is unique for each person, and it is the invitation for all.

Now, four years later, here I was in a small village in Portugal, working through my process. Guided by Spirit with answers for myself and experiences that were healing my heart and others that joined me each week for the Collective. I had already completed my Essential Ecosystem Experience, focused on stabilizing the natural body and vessel, and was now deeply within the Empress level. This next step explores the essence and how this new life wants to be built. I was asking myself, *What I do want to see in the world? What is my legacy and who am I becoming in this co-creation?* It was the culmination of the Ecosystem within the third-dimensional reality of every day. Within the Empress journey, I was witnessing what wanted to arise in my essence, realizing all I could be. One of the keys I discovered was that I really have to know and trust myself and others around me. Who are your partners in life? Do they have your back?

One fatal evening at the beginning of June 2023, I got a call. It was Nathan. We hadn't spoken in over three months.

"Hey." He began. "Howzit?" A very common and casual way we Southern Africans speak.

"Fine," I said flatly.

"I wanted to let you know, before anyone else called, that I think I met someone."

"Oh, that's nice."

"She's amazing," he gushed. "A nurse. She's not like us and a little crazy, but we spent four hours together and then another thirty-six hours, and it could be love." He continued with joyful glee to share the details of their date as I sat in utter amazement. A total of forty hours and he was already talking about love? To me?

"She said that she understands my issues, Lizete. She understands how I suffer from complex PTSD. She says that I'm definitely on the autism spectrum and she totally gets why I've been struggling to build healthy relationships."

"Wow, that's so nice to be understood," I said dryly.

Chapter Ten — Compassion: The Leadership of Christed Consciousness

I'd understood him too, from the very first call, yet I had never labeled him. I had always known I had the gift and tools to totally recover the conditions of his traumatized essence. At least I had the faith I did and willing to put all my time and effort into his healing. When, reaching the end of my rope, I did dare to label him, he attacked me with all fury.

"And how is the intimacy going?" I asked hesitantly.

The reply was ruthless. "Best ever. No problem whatsoever. She really turns me on."

"Oh, that's nice. So at least now you know that the problem wasn't you,"

"Yep. I'm all good. I didn't have a problem after all."

"So, all our issues were simply that I wasn't sexy enough for you."

"Exactly!" He sounded relieved.

I smiled. "Intimacy wasn't a problem for us early on either," I made him recall.

"I'm not calling to talk about us. Just letting you know that there is no us, and I've definitely moved on. I encourage you to do the same. You have some real issues, Lizete. You are so deep and sensitive. Truly, you are too much."

"That's so funny." Cool as a cucumber. "I thought that I just wasn't enough. At least that is what you continuously said in all the different ways."

"That's it. That's what I'm trying to say. Our love wasn't real."

What? Our love wasn't real?

I had heard enough. Hanging up the phone, not willing to hear another word, I surrendered immediately into Spirit. I didn't want to make up a story. I didn't want to bypass this pain. I didn't want to push his hurtful words under the carpet. I wanted the truth. I had learned there is no way to escape it. Around and around it goes, so let us deal with it right here and now.

Spirit guided me to the fireplace, and I crumbled on a small carpet, all strength abandoning my limbs. On my hands and knees, I allowed myself to feel into all of it. The emotional pain was the most intense I had ever felt in my life. It was brutal. It was cruel. I allowed the cry of my soul to release out of my mouth as a scream of a wounded animal that shock me to the core. Blood started running from my nose as a reaction to the shattering rupture happening in my mind as my mouth channeled, "You dare to betray Lilith!" It was a question, a statement, a terrifying scream that echoed in every cell. I had tapped into something ancient.

Who was Lilith?

Nathan had said he hoped to be friends, but in the following days, I knew that this would not be possible. He kept talking about how he had never wanted to hurt me, but he was following his truth. His truth? This was new. We had never, in four years, spoken of individual truth, only the quest of the truth.

And then, in a long message, I could see how the story had changed in his narrative. "I did love you very much. But you were simply not the one. I wouldn't have wanted to be with anyone else at the time."

This was the difference. When he had promised to spend our lifetime together, build our home and family together, to love me always, he didn't actually mean it. He only meant that was what he felt, in the moment. "At the time!" That is truly the difference. It wasn't meant to be a foundation to build my life upon, like I had been made to believe.

What is a person's truth truly worth when they have broken every single promise? What is the purpose of this truth? It was clear. He

Chapter Ten — Compassion: The Leadership of Christed Consciousness

was an expert in getting his needs met. He had traded a transformative healer in for a nurse who didn't need him to heal nor maintain a standard to do so. He was gone, and I was left with pain, grief, and wounds of betrayal.

He had betrayed Lilith. Another key was being offered.

Spirit led me to read about Lilith. I was being taken back to the origins. According to esoteric text, Lilith was known as the original woman in the garden, or the first wife of Adam. As the story went, she was expelled from the Garden because she refused to be dominated by Adam. After being rejected and abandoned, she retreated into a cave, and then took her revenge by becoming a terrifying demoness.

Or so the story went.

I could understand her. In this moment I could see how while a woman in love truly does want nothing other than harmony and peace with her beloved, how is she to submit to a man when he is not in alignment with divine consciousness? When he is choosing chaos, conflict, and confusion? Why would she? It is complete self-destruction. Is that not suicide of the soul? I also knew from Lilith's example that the answer was not to retaliate or seek revenge, as any such action would be fruitless and dark. I felt the rage. I understood and wept the tears of frustration. Alone in my dungeon of death, I died again and again.

Once again Spirit asked me, in light of all this, if I was willing to forgive. "Yes, Spirit," I replied. "I seek only love."

One night I wanted to tell him this. He didn't answer the phone. I called again. He declined. I must have called twelve times. This was the one and only time I tested the last promise he had made me: "I will always answer you no matter where I am." He had broken his last promise. I was alone and my journey of forgiveness was only between me and Abba. I would get no closure. I would get no last goodbye. So, into the void I went.

People who knew us as a couple have reflected to me that Nathan got off easy. They cringe when I say that I have forgiven him. But this is only because they don't understand what forgiveness truly is, and how it is the key to true compassion and our spiritual power.

To forgive is not to agree, nor to condone. It is not saying that what happened was okay in any shape or form. Forgiveness is the step we take to choose to accept what has happened in reality, agree with Spirit to actually learn the lesson being provided, and then evolve into the higher version of ourselves.

To claim our freedom, we have to set everyone else free. Even from the promises that they made. I needed to understand why our relationship fell apart to make peace within myself. I needed to see where I had deluded myself into letting this occur.

I was taken to the beginning of the end: the moment in the garden when man and woman—who had been in unity and peace with God, walking in their divine consciousness—fell.

THE THREE CURSES

Genesis 3:10–13: "'I heard your voice in the garden,' the man answered, 'and I was afraid because I was naked, so I hid from you.'

"'Who told you that you are naked?' God asked. 'Did you eat fruit from the tree that I commanded you not to eat?'

"The man answered, 'The woman whom you provided for me gave me fruit from the tree, and I ate some of it.'

"Then the Lord God asked the woman, 'What did you do?'

"'The Shining One misled me,' the woman answered, 'so I ate.'"

Whether the story of the fall is allegory, parable, or actual history

Chapter Ten — Compassion: The Leadership of Christed Consciousness

does not matter from the point of consciousness. It is the story that lays the foundation for all of humanity, which is the "fallen" state we are all healing from in our evolution and ascension to divine consciousness. It is the story ingrained in our cells and DNA from generations past. It is not to be escaped, but alchemized and transformed from within. This is the journey I have done within myself.

What I notice in particular as I reread this verse is the understanding that man realized he was naked. Exposed, vulnerable, and ashamed of his natural state before the God that had never accused, judged, or criticized. The divine came asking a question and encountered shame. Shame is the lowest frequency and the fruit of knowing good and evil. They, our ancestors, had become aware of their true state. They were no longer "perfect" in their own perspective, so their attitude changed. The Essential Ecosystem experience showed me how to walk in right standing with Spirit rather than submitting to any dogmatic understanding of how I need to present to stand in divine presence. I had to accept I was loved just for who I am, a person who makes mistakes and is loved unconditionally, through Christ.

The second thing I notice is that neither man or woman took accountability for what happened, nor their individual choices. Man blamed God and woman. God had made her, and she had deceived him. She had convinced him to take of the fruit. It was her fault.

Woman also avoided responsibility. She blamed the Shining One. At that moment, both of them could have asked for forgiveness. Neither of them did. This was their downfall. They didn't believe, even after all the goodness God had showed them, that God was able to forgive. As a result of this choice, three curses were given: three results from the original separation between humankind and the divine as we were exiled from the Garden of Eden.

The revelation of this for me was an understanding that Abba, the divine, is love. Removing us from the Garden was grace—not a punishment. If we had eaten of the tree of life in a corrupted state, we would live forever in a body and form that was now contaminated with separation, disease, and death. The frequencies of shame, fear, guilt, and apathy had taken root.

When we look at these curses from the neutral lens of consciousness, we can begin to understand all distortions that play out in our reality, even up to today. This is the skeleton key to unlocking the foundation of peace and abundance. The Essential Ecosystem offered me this new perspective, and I understood why exactly it had brought me into alignment with the natural divinity I was now enjoying.

I invite you now, dear reader, to read these words, to discover these curses with fresh eyes. Not as a story outside of yourself, but as a window into the infinite potential you hold as a soul created in the image of God, the infinite Source of all that is. How can you apply this to the circumstances playing out in your life? How does this illuminate your next steps through space and time? Can you forgive? Be forgiven? Return to the garden as the Christ within you?

INDEPENDENCE /CONSCIOUSNESS
The Three Curses We Are Healing

CURSE OF ADAM	SELF-DOUBT
Air Element / Sovereignty	*Survival focus, drained life force*
CURSE OF EVE	SELF-SACRIFICE
Water Element / Sacred Service	*Desire belongs to husband, heart to children*
CURSE OF THE SNAKE	SELF-SABOTAGE
Earth Element / Security	*Control, manipulation, demonizing personal power*

The Curse of the Snake

Genesis 3:14–15: "The Lord God told the Shining One, 'Because you have done this, you are more cursed than all the livestock, and more than all the earth's animals, you'll crawl on your belly and eat dust as long as you live. I'll place hostility between you and the woman, between your offspring and her offspring. He'll strike you on the head, and you'll strike him on the heel.'"

The curse of the Shining One was a fall from grace. The snake went from one who was revered in the garden with free rein, who may have even been lord of the animal kingdom, to one cursed to be below every animal and move on its belly. This tells me that the snake did not always slither on the ground, but once had full dominion over all elements, or at least moved upright.

This calls to mind the dragon, a creature that has been known in many civilizations but that has lost its grace, power, and authority. The dragon, now reduced to myth and legend, is the only creature that roamed Earth, breathed fire, swam in the oceans, and flew in the skies. Today we have the lion as the king of the jungle and also the primal symbol of Jeshua. However, before that, it may well have been the dragon. The rest of the animal kingdom has not fallen, they suffer only because man and woman forgot their place as guardians, and the dragon who preserved their dignity and glory is not empowered to defend them.

The dragon is representative of primal force. This is the innate intelligence of the natural human body. The intuitive and instinctual senses and perception that allow us to make moment-by-moment choices of wisdom and balance. It is the power of life force that animates us. We have access to it through our energetic body and is the state of enlightenment.

This Essential Ecosystem taught me, just as Hawkins highlighted in his table of frequencies, that peace comes before enlightenment. We need to make peace with our light and our divinity. We need to honor the snake within us that has pretended, failed, run away, projected, and slithered in jealousy. It is the work of divine alchemy to choose to redeem that part of ourselves. Once we do this for ourselves, we cultivate not only the light and the primal force that regenerates our being, but compassion for the other. We overcome our fear and codependency, embrace ourselves, and become empowered to take our next step. We have been conditioned out of our power and taught to fear our own light. Yet the snake, symbol of health and vitality, is within us.

The Curse of Eve

Genesis 3:16: "He told the woman, 'I'll greatly increase the pain of your labor during childbirth. It will be painful for you to bear children, since your trust is turning toward your husband, and he will dominate you.'"

The curse toward women—or Lilith as the first woman—was twofold. Firstly, her pain would increase in childbearing. Secondly, she would be dominated by her husband.

After I was married at age twenty-one, it took about two years before my parents and other relatives started asking when we were going to have children. My first husband would have been an excellent father and was excited at the prospect. I, on the other hand, was hesitant as I was very young and my career was just beginning.

The support I'd have was minimal; my parents were far away, and the demands of life were draining. If I had children, I would have to put them into daycare, and that wasn't the scenario I had

Chapter Ten — Compassion: The Leadership of Christed Consciousness

imagined for myself. I wanted to raise my children myself, know them, guide them, and teach them. I didn't see how I could do that and felt that, at twenty-three that I was not set up to win in this construct of society.

One day, I asked Spirit to show me what it actually meant to have a child. The image they showed shook me. I saw myself on a surgical slab. The surgeons created a slit from the base of my neck down to just below my heart. They removed my beating heart and placed it in the hands of an infant, about two years old. The cute little one received it with two open hands and gleefully ran out of the room.

The revelation was graphic, but I completely understood what they meant. In the fallen state, when we have a child, we literally love that child so much that our heart is never truly our own again. It doesn't beat in our own chests anymore. Wherever that child goes, and whatever free will choice they make, we as mothers will always be impacted. I recognized my mother's heart and her pain. Her worry whenever I made a trip or was stepping out in the unknown. My heart broke for us women everywhere.

Having a child is the greatest love a woman can possibly know, and thankfully, women do it successfully all the time. The arrival of my beloved nephew, Gabriel, on May 18, 2024 was the most glorious and wonderful event to happen in my family.

One day, as I sat feeding him, looking into his beautiful face, and feeling his presence, I could only weep with joy, awe, and reverence at the amazing miracle of life and innocence. When my sister called in tears, telling me that he had hurt himself and fractured his knee, her pain pulled at the deepest recesses of my soul.

There is a solution for this, but it is in understanding that we are never separate. The waters in my sister are in him, and they are always in communication in the field. Yet mother and child are in separate and different vessels. She cannot protect him enough, except by her faith and love. He will live his life. He will make his choices. He has free will. For her to know peace and the love for her son, she has to trust God enough to know that her child is loved and protected.

The second curse of woman is that she would be dominated by her husband. I had been dominated consciously twice in my life, and unconsciously for a lot of it. First, by my father, who always had something to say about every action, word, and gesture. Mainly it was well-intentioned and presented as my education, but a lot of it was about not being an embarrassment to him. I was never free or trusted to be myself. I needed a lot of forgiveness as I reclaimed my power and grew up.

Second, I was dominated by Nathan. It is one thing to be dominated by one who is following the way of compassion and another who is cold and unkind. Lilith is not necessarily a different woman than Eve. "Eve" was the name that Adam gave his wife after the fall. But imagine the pain of a naturally divine ancient being, connected to divine consciousness, now chained underneath the command of a mortal who, if confused, chaotic, and in turmoil, could make the rules up as they went along. The healing of this curse is to reclaim our direct connection with the divine. Each in our own body. To be true to what is real, good, and true in each moment.

This is honoring and healing the feminine, and her most important choice is who she chooses to partner and spend time with. We still love our partners and men; however, we are no longer subject to their whims and desires. Side by side is the template and that requires both men and women to be free to choose.

We are elevating our ability to love in freedom and healing our heartbreak of separation. Love is always present, and it is the only commodity that multiplies the more we give it away. If the other doesn't treat you with the respect you need, you need to find the courage, healing, and strength to love yourself first and fill your own cup to share with others. We are healing not-enoughness, for ourselves and for the whole paradigm of our reality. With love and the divine feminine, there is always only more.

The Curse of Adam

Genesis 3:17–19: "He told the man, 'Because you have listened to what your wife said, and have eaten from the tree about which I commanded you, "You are not to eat from it," cursed is the ground because of you. You'll eat from it through pain-filled labor for the rest of your life. It will produce thorns and thistles for you, and you'll eat the plants from the meadows. You will eat food by the sweat of your brow until you're buried in the ground, because you were taken from it. You're made from dust, and you'll return to dust.'"

The curse toward Adam, the first man, was not disconnection from the divine, as the relationship continued even outside of Eden for all the nine-hundred-plus years of his life. The disconnection was from the easeful and abundant life he had experienced in the garden. The disconnection from the true Mother, the Garden of Eden. Now he had to toil for his sustenance; he had to work for his food. He would have to work to survive for the first time. Everything he created would no longer flow naturally and effortlessly, but would have to be manifested with hard labor and conflict.

This was one of the things that never allowed my love to flourish with Nathan. He was always working. Busy with his mind, using his hands, or pushing his body. For love to flow, there has to be an active presence of stillness to receive. Love is invisible. To be seen and known, we have to be still enough to feel it.

Adam also lost something else that day. Something that has remained hidden and undervalued for all this stretch of time. He lost the wise council of his beloved. He no longer trusted her insights, her predictions, or the access to divine knowing that courses through her being. Adam lost his intimate companion that day—the day he no longer trusted her.

WE ARE THE SEED

Another revelation that came through was that I, and we, are all three: man (masculine), woman (feminine), and Shining One (snake/kundalini life force) are all within us. We are one. We all have the masculine side within us. This is our active part that puts things into the manifest physical world and makes the final decision. We all have the feminine side within us. This is the one who whispers with Spirit and understands the secrets in the simple and mundane things of life. We are the snake embodying life force through what we think, say, and do, actively creating our experience by co-creating with the field that I call Spirit. Within the ARISE Academy, we explore this consciousness as we embody evolution step by step as we gather every week to walk together in Christ Consciousness.

All these insights came through many moments sitting in the silence of my cave and dungeon, replaying the moments in the Garden, the pain of the loss. I had no choice but to surrender to the burning flame of desire and the embarrassment of Nathan's cruel discarding. I had not been chosen. I was too much. I was not enough. Yes, I understood Lilith, but I did not fear her. I understood her pain.

Chapter Ten — Compassion: The Leadership of Christed Consciousness

CO-CREATING IN THE NEW WORLD
Moving Toward Wholeness

Masculine Polarity   **Feminine Polarity**

AIR ELEMENT — Mental Body — First Dimension — **Gratitude**

SPACE ELEMENT — Light Body — Fifth Dimension — **Grace**

WATER ELEMENT — Emotional Body — Second Dimension — **Gentleness**

FIRE ELEMENT — Energetic Body — Fourth Dimension — **Growth**

EARTH ELEMENT — Physcial Body — Third Dimension — **Grit**

I cannot be an Eve. I don't want to be with anyone who needs to dominate me. I have no need to rule over anyone, so why should anyone rule over me? We are meant to walk side by side with our partners. The words from the very first channel I had ever received from the Jeshua and the collective of guides returned to me:

The suffering we feel
is the imbalance.
This was not the plan or the design.

The design is perfect.
Do you not have eyes to see?

Then have ears to hear.
The design is perfect.
You and I are the design, beautiful one,
who is so loved, so loved,
so loved, by the whole universe.

There is no one
to channel anymore
when the soul remembers it is God-consciousness embodied.
You are the highest authority on the face of the Earth.

You are free by your very existence, beloved,
and yet you are not above another being.
Do you understand this?
Honor life and choose love.
Be whole again.
Do what it takes to recover every piece of
your soul that has been left behind,
and come home.

Nathan was free to change his mind. He was free to fall in love again. Why not? That is his free will choice. I had so much compassion for him. Yet what I found was that in all my giving of compassion and love to him, I had absolutely forgotten to extend that compassion to myself.

This is where the journey begins, beloved. That is the whole

Chapter Ten — Compassion: The Leadership of Christed Consciousness

purpose of this book. The whole path in a nutshell, or a seed. We are the seed. Each and every one of us. We have all we need in the natural order of things to thrive. We must create the container for ourselves so that we are empowered to love others. I had to remember who I was. I had to extend compassion to myself. I had to understand that my purpose and value is to give and receive. We have been taught to use our love in a way that is self-destructive, and it was time for something new.

I processed the grief, using the very steps we are learning in this book to alchemize my suffering into light and joy. To turn my rage and anger into peace. To release the pain of my pride and start to use my newfound passion to create instead of destroy. I realized that the most forgiveness I had to do was in forgiving myself. I had trusted blindly. I had followed without hesitation. I didn't look out for my needs; I trusted they would be taken care of. Now, as I sat with all my broken pieces in my hands, I realized what I had done.

I had betrayed myself.

I had dared betray Lilith. I had turned woman into a maid, a beggar of affection, a negotiator with a man of hollow promises.

Nathan treated me as common and replaceable because I had handed myself over as if that were true. He didn't understand my love because he didn't have any for me. That is not a reflection of me. It is my responsibility to take care of me. I am not a victim. I am a daughter of God. All women are. We are naturally divine, but we have been taught systemically to betray ourselves. And we will do so until we learn to never do it again by practicing compassion not just for the other, but for ourselves as well.

I had learned to open the door to love. First in accepting Jeshua into my life at seventeen and second when I loved Nathan the way that I did: unconditionally. As he was, with no labels. It is another mastery to learn to close the door. The day he said our love was not real, I felt an ancient, massive door in the cosmos. I felt the door move, a spooky, creaking sound reverberating in my soul, and then it swung shut with a bang. This was a door that had not been closed for eons. As a woman, I was finding my balance. Claiming my power. Why would I want a man who cannot love me?

THE LINE IN THE SAND REVEALED

One night, Jeshua called my attention to a familiar scripture piece: John 8:3–11. This is where a woman caught in adultery is brought before Jesus. Her accusers said, "Teacher, this woman has been caught in the very act of adultery. Now in the Law, Moses commanded us to stone such women to death. What do you say?"

His reply? "Let the person among you who is without sin be the first to throw a stone at her." All the accusers left. Jeshua did not make the move to defend her or save her, he only reflected the light on her accusers to see if, within their own hearts, they were without sin.

From my revelation, "sin" means that one is separate from divine consciousness and right standing. When someone truly is honest with themselves, they would never accuse anyone of anything. Their own consciousness convicts them; they too are not perfect. In our true consciousness, we step into grace and dare not judge another lest we too are judged. This is also compassion in action.

Christ Consciousness only works for those who are willing to admit they have done wrong themselves. No accusation is necessary, nor is there any need to wait around for an apology. I've made mistakes too. Now, sitting through my own healing, I noticed that in my relationship, I had been so committed in healing him that I believed once he was well, everything would be fine. I completely ignored the healing that I had to do. Completely denied my own wounds and traumas that had been left without love.

Though he could not love me the way that I wanted, he did open my heart. He taught me how deeply I can love. He showed me what a gift and joy it was to open my heart. And that is the greatest gift in the world.

Compassion is a powerful step. It begins with having compassion for yourself first. Your divinity and humanity. Your gifts and needs. Your strengths and preferences. When you are willing to give of yourself only to those who can receive you, no one else is needed. All you need to do is trust that. True compassionate, leadership is being around people who understand the situation. They understand that you are on a journey, and they trust you are doing the best you can. These are the people I now build my life with every day. For those who choose to judge instead, there is simply no time. Though once I held these people tightly, I now allow them to drift away as they follow their sacred journey.

A LINE IN THE SAND
(A LETTER TO END THE LOVE OF A LIFETIME)

You used me. And that's okay.

I kept you company while you could do "better" for yourself. Your love was not real. That's okay too. I know it's not personal. That is yours to use as you wish.

My love was real, and this love actually healed me in ways I didn't even know a person could be broken. You tried to break me. My spirit, my heart, my mind, making me feel daily how I was not enough. To me? Who only ever extended you love?

I love you. Oh, wait, I'm not sure. Oh, I don't … then I do, I do, I do. My whole life hanging in surrender in your hands. In mid-construction in the middle of a jungle with no defense. This was devotion. Trust. Love. Faith. Family. This was a powerful courageous woman submitting all to receive love. And getting only breadcrumbs and a few battle scars in return.

You almost got away with it, too. Using my faith in love, my faith in God, and my faith in humans against my own self and wellbeing, you led me to death only for me to find I am natural divinity. The real power of my gift which you mocked and now will serve many. You threw me away and treated me as if I was garbage. And I let you do it, too. Over and over.

To heal, I had to forgive you. To be whole, I had to forgive myself. It is now done. You were not the only to have hurt me, but you were the one that triggered every wound. I may have done the same for you.

Yesterday marked six years since we connected. It has forever changed my life. I am forever grateful and done.

This journey has led me home. To me.

Thank you for the training. The manipulation I was blind to. The lies of the mouth. The seduction of incremental improvement. The true power of choice. To know when the dream and vision is false or truly seen. It has to do with truth. Not mine, yours, or hers, dear mortal.

But the one who shows itself in all of time.

I hope all is working out for you. I know the story is that you were left and abandoned. But we know, bubs. Leaving you was the hardest thing I have ever done, but you made staying impossible. And returning would have been suicide with the way you treated me.

The war is over.

Love is not combative. It is unconditional. Each has their way of finding this. Take care, soldier, and safe travels.

Always,

L

PART IV:
ARISE

Unlocking Legacy

Time is always moving forward, or so it seems—at least in our everyday waking consciousness. Each day, we get to awaken to new opportunities, move forward, change directions, make new choices, and experience new things. What I hope you receive from this book, and this work, is the remembrance that with each new thing, there is also that which has always been to consider—often unseen, taken for granted, and dismissed.

As new solutions and technologies come online, it is imperative that we understand, as humanity, that what has worked for millions of years in perfect order will always work. We are fully supported by an intelligent life-force technology found in the natural, biological, and energetic universe ... *if* we are willing to learn from it. It is our natural divinity that sustains us; however, we have the free will to shape our reality in the now moment.

By sharing this personal and vulnerable story, I do not speak as one who has attained, but as one who came to the frightening and scary conclusion that I knew nothing and was left only with the choice to be willing to listen. Indeed, my house of cards came crumbling down—but in losing everything, in the death and destruction of that construct, an eternal essence was found. It is not easy to face the fact that we don't have all the answers, but this process ensures that we have and can create the stillness to connect to the voice within—and that voice that *does* have the answer right now, for the very next step.

I hope these experiences I have shared and how these revelations were shown does not lay an expectation or standard for you that hinders. My journey is not your journey; it only serves as an example to support you to trust your own courage and lean in to your own consciousness. To create the space to experience your own amazing, incredible, never before seen genius, as it emerges from the essence that we each are learning ourselves to be.

We have all been programmed in many ways, and programs are not a bad thing. They are the way that intelligence organizes itself. Some programs are fundamental and natural, but many that I am addressing through these stories and experiences are also the ones that kept us stuck in a cycle of abuse, pain and suffering. It is truly a journey for each of us to choose for ourselves that which is right, good, and true. However, it is with paradoxical programming, especially that which goes against our very nature, is where this work most applies. This is the need for alchemy and transformation: not to transform our essence, but to peel away the layers of what we never were in the first place.

In this journey of surrender, I found myself often faced with constraints and concerns about money. How was I going to afford to survive and still take the space and time to heal myself? However, it was in that surrender that support came. Everything I truly needed was provided for. No one could fix me, because I needed to find the way that I would "fix" myself. To make peace within my own consciousness, and in doing so, find the regenerative aspect within my being that reconstructs anew. You have this within you too, dear one. It will be in your unique form, according to your beautiful gifts and special talents. I just hope that you know you do indeed have it all within you.

I experience my body now as the great adventure. Carrying thirty kilos of excess weight for over two decades, I can not begin to describe how living feels in this new body—and your body can do this too. My creations, including this book, the retreats and the programs I co-create within the ARISE Academy are my leadership legacy. This is what I will be leaving behind for the next generations, for the collective that will follow. My voice is what I found in silence as I sang my soul alchemy songs, healed my heart, and navigated the void for these three and half years. You, too, are called to find your unique brand of genius and express. The more you believe in the value of that essence, the more you will guided step by step to bring that into form.

When we awaken to our gifts, it can be very disorienting and frightening. We don't know where we are going, who we are going to become, or how to connect as we used to. I hope these stories give you the hope and faith that you will truly be alright, even as you continue to evolve. Even when you are lost in the forest, know that the moon, the sky, the trees, and the soil know exactly where you are.

You can take this time to heal. You are loved. That is really the only seed we truly have to hold on to. There is no dogma or religion about it.

In a world that seems cold, indifferent, and enormous, the biggest question that comes up for people is, "If God is good, why is there so much suffering?" I am not exempt of this suffering, and yet I still know that God is good. We have to find that love, the goodness, and that faith inside of ourselves. That is truly the miraculous—because in that grace and embrace, we find that are never alone, we are never forgotten, and we will always have a place in this world.

ARISE, friend. For we are building the new.

CHAPTER ELEVEN

Welcome to Everyday Eden

Thank you, dear one, for joining me on this epic journey through our process of the Essential Ecosystem for Everyday Eden. We have now completed the twelve steps walking through the pathways of the three pillars of awareness, activation, and alignment, I and the Collective have journeyed for the last four years, in order to ignite our natural divinity. The evolution continues.

In this next step of our journey, we will explore what makes it all coalesce and truly come together. The key to building momentum for Everyday Eden lies in one simple distinction and understanding: there are no villains in our story. No, not one!

DELIVER YOURSELF FROM VICTIMHOOD

Most stories we have programmed into consciousness offer a clear "good guy" and "bad guy." We are now elevating into a higher, more constructive, and more empowered understanding. As beings who hold the power of free will, we have been given the ultimate gift of having a yes and a no.

This duality is part of the divine construct of our reality. Duality, or the two sides of the coin, was initially designed to create balance. The day and night. The yin and yang. Man and woman. The two operating together, in harmony, side by side, so that there could be a new form—one whole singular manifestation. It is how form is created. However, the lower matrix of consciousness has used this duality to create the separation that causes all suffering and distortion. Within this third-dimensional construct, if there is a villain, there must be a victim!

And then by default, there needs to be a savior.

The ultimate cage! This is the one thing we need rescuing from, and you alone are the warrior that is here to do that for you. This is the core message I have learned from my master, my guide, my King and my Lord, Jeshua.

As I am, so are you in this world.

I have shared how Jeshua has been revealed to me as the Messiah, and indeed whom I believe personally to be the savior of humanity. Serving as a wayshower, a bridge and sacrificial lamb, so that all that may believe and can once again have communion with God. Or, as I have called it, so all may claim their natural divinity.

What sets Him apart from all other masters that have come before Him or after, is not the miracles He created during His lifetime. It is not only the life and leadership He displayed within His mastery and everyday example, but most profoundly for me, what happened as He hung on the cross, just before death.

One of the first revelations I had of the cross was the fact He was judged to death without doing a single thing wrong. If you have never read the actual words about the crucifixion, I encourage you to not turn away. It is difficult to face, but it was done with you in mind. He was judged to die for absolutely no reason or fault, except that He refused to give up His identity as the son of God and His belief in being one with God. This is what He died for. He represented the essence of freedom of choice and refused to give up His spiritual identity. Imagine being killed for an idea—He had harmed no one.

In doing so, He purchased this very thing for all 0f us. The very last words He choose to leave us in His earthly incarnation are found in the gospel of Luke 23:33–35: "When they came to the place called the Skull, they crucified him there, along with the criminals—one on his right, the other on his left. Jesus said, 'Father, forgive them, for they do not know what they are doing.' And they divided up his clothes by casting lots.

"The people stood watching, and the rulers even sneered at him. They said, 'He saved others; let him save himself if he is God's Messiah, the Chosen One.'"

Even in the moment of death, pain unimaginable and injustice that would break any soul, He chose forgiveness. He chose to love. He understood His role and was willing to accept it fully. In doing this, He overcame the ultimate villain and reclaimed all power over the realm of darkness and evil. He never saw Himself as a victim.

This is what gives Him the unique role as savior. He offers this salvation to each and every soul that will open the door of the heart. He stated that He came for all who would accept Him as He stands and knocks at the door of every heart.

John 3:16: "For this is how God loved the world: He gave his uniquely existing Son so that everyone who believes in him would not be lost but have eternal life."

The purpose of His life and entire ministry was that we may have eternal life in Him. The Christ Consciousness that grants us the regeneration possible within our natural divinity. This is the energetic and spiritual inheritance of each human being if we choose it. He came to restore us to Eden, serving as the final sacrifice to break the curse made in the Garden in the beginning.

The role of savior is uniquely His.

He also said on the cross, John 19:30: "When he had received the drink, Jesus said, 'It is finished.' With that, he bowed his head and gave up his spirit."

"It is finished." As He said it, the curtain that separated the people from the Holy of Holies in the temple, was ripped from bottom to top, signifying that the way is made open and available for us all. This is the foundation of the gospel, or the good news.

Is this religious? No. For the work was so complete there is no need left for any religion, clergy, or ceremony. There is no intermediary required nor needed to give us access to that which is a given as a complete gift of grace. It cannot be contained in one building, book, or organization. It is free. It is personal. It is individual choice. It is a spiritual and energetic covenant to reconnect with and receive the communion of our highest Christed essence.

It is our choice to cultivate a life of meaning, guided by love and harmony. That is the essence of the teaching of the Essential Ecosystem of Everyday Eden. It is the frequency and the mastery we are cultivating within the ARISE Academy.

If we can accept by faith and grace that the Savior has come for you and I, and establish this as the first dimension, we then find that the second dimension is that of duality. The victim and the villain! This dance to choose to live and discern what is evil. "Evil" is "live" in reverse, which could be interpreted as evil being the opposite of what is good, right, and true. This is the dynamic of choice we are navigating in each step through space and time. Hence our focus on multidimensional mastery as how we navigate through our individual timeline.

One of the most helpful constructs of thought, given to me during my time in the jungle, came from another master, Buddha.

Under the bodhi tree, the Buddha sat and meditated for seven weeks until he attained enlightenment. One of his realizations was that there is only one of us here. I, too, had been shown that the concept of the Universe, that every individual is participating and co-creating in their own unique experience of reality. We each navigate through space and time with reality reflecting back not what we want, as we discussed at the beginning of this book, but who we are being.

This brings us to the understanding of how reality works as a mirror. If we are busy putting blame or shame on people outside of ourselves, we are automatically abdicating responsibility and losing power. When we hold up the mirror—actually looking at reality—we can observe, learn from our mistakes, and evolve. This is not an easy lesson to grasp, but when we do, we become truly free to mold and shape reality with the power of our co-creation.

Responsibility takes on new meaning. It becomes my ability to respond.

As I have shared these ideas with others in the past, they looked at me questioningly—could multidimensional mastery be so simple? But simple does not mean easy. Just the other day, a member of the ARISE Collective stated, "Who knew that claiming our power would be this hard?"

It is the most challenging and courageous thing we can ever do with our life. It is a choice of mastery. But likewise, most certainly, it is the most rewarding and fulfilling path. Both in this life and the one that awaits, just beyond the veil in eternity, where our soul returns, once this earthly life is over.

Death is the surest thing in life. The beautiful paradox. When we make peace with it in the here and now, it loses its power as the opposite of life and becomes a doorway to understanding there is no end. Only eternity.

PEACE WITH WHO YOU ARE

The other question I get, especially from people who come from religion, is, "Does the devil exist?"

The devil is the ultimate villain, and I do not deny his existence, as Jeshua also did not. He is called the father of lies, and sacred scripture says that he comes to steal, kill, and destroy. What we need to realize is that he is the same as the lower matrix of reality, and only has the power that we personally attribute to him. As human beings, we were given ultimate dominion, power, and control over the Earth and every creepy-crawly that walks on the Earth.

The first time I had this awareness was when I entered the church after my first out-of-body experience, in the park at age seventeen. I had heard a lot about the devil, but I realized then that if he had any real power over me, or if I belonged to him in any way, he or his legions of demons would have simply been able to stop me from giving my life to Jesus out of free will.

So, as we can clearly see, although he may appear powerful, he has nothing on Jeshua. He is a deceiver. Our fear of him and our need to survive this mortal life feed his dominion. Many believe that we can sell our souls to the devil. Indeed, we can choose who we worship, and there are many who have chosen to voluntarily give themselves to him, but we cannot really sell what is not ours. Remember, Jeshua purchased our soul, and it ultimately belongs to God. What we give up in any contract we make is our free will, and eventually—without fail—we will pay the price.

We get to choose. This is our power.

When I first joined the church at seventeen, I had a poster of a woman that I was connected to. She had smoky white eyes, snakes in her hair, and a necklace around her neck with the word "Li." I resonated with her somehow and placed her picture above my bed. Her eyes were piercing, and over a short period of time she started to gain more and more energetic and spiritual power. She seemed to look intensely at anyone who entered my room.

My parents, who joined the church shortly after me, started worrying that there was a demon in the house, hiding behind the poster. At the time, my best friend Paula's mother was a gifted medium. I had sat many times in circle with them as entities came through and spoke to us. I never felt uncomfortable with them, but there was a darkness about these transmissions. I noticed that their advice would give me one step forward and three steps back. I understand it so much better today. The source may not have been Christed and purified, but I was magnetically drawn to it as I, too, carried a gift of being an open channel and medium—and it met me at the frequency I was in.

One day, my pastor and his wife were invited to my house to see the poster. They both agreed that there was a demon behind the poster and an entity that was communicating. They ordered me to tear it up. Everything inside me said no. I knew that Li, who I understand today was Lilith speaking to me already, was not evil, simply misunderstood. She had traversed eons of time of oppression, rejection, persecution, hiding, and judgment, and she had the potential to heal the whole Earth as she represents the first woman and the essence of the divine feminine in its natural divine order of creation.

They were so convinced it was evil and insisted that if I wanted to belong to the church, I needed to choose between her or Jesus, as the two were incompatible. Light and dark. I had no doubt in my mind about following Jeshua, but under this pressure, against my will and my internal knowing, it felt wrong.

I took the picture within my hands and tore up her up into little pieces. I regretted it instantly.

This was me betraying Lilith.

This was me betraying women and setting the course to have to find the light and all the pieces of my soul back.

This all because of one thing. Though their fear of the devil was strong, what was stronger was their fear of my personal and spiritual power.

That is our essence and most valuable commodity! Yet, the whole world is busy distracting you from it and setting up roadblocks. Fear is what feeds the devil and that is why in the ARISE Academy, we don't deny his existence. But we also understand that our choice is to follow Jeshua, and just like him, our mastery is one: to know and live the freedom of love.

We each are responsible to ensure Satan has nothing in us. This means that there is nothing in our conscience that we have not made peace with. If we create a villain, if we create this great and fearful enemy in our consciousness, we have chained ourselves to a life that is a constant and continuous hardship of spiritual warfare. And unfortunately, our beliefs will manifest. The students and masters within the ARISE Academy are not interested in chasing and casting out demons in others.

We are invested in creating the power of Christ in our consciousness. Where we are so clear and purified, that the devil has no dominion to rule over us. We do this by acknowledging that we have the lower four frequencies within us: apathy, guilt, regret, and shame.

Every human born after the fall has these codes within their DNA, as the sins (or the separation from divine consciousness) of the fathers are visited up the children to the third or fourth generation. But we can use the ARISE process of alchemy to transform these frequencies

Chapter Eleven — Welcome to Everyday Eden

into the higher frequencies of neutrality, joy, love, and peace. The frequencies that are in resonance with everything that is naturally aligned to be life-giving and affirming to regeneration and natural divinity.

It is incredibly liberating to know that we need not challenge the power of the realm of darkness. It has no hold on us as we remain in the grace, love, and peace of the Holy Spirit, the Spirit of Wholeness.

My greatest example for all spiritual warfare in our life was given in scripture as Jeshua was called to fast and pray in the desert for forty days and forty nights.

While fasting can bring us closer to Spirit, Jeshua was not seeking the face of God in this instance. He had that connection and presence daily and was in permanent communication with Abba. He walked in and carried the enlightenment from Spirit in His everyday life. He was facing His final test in preparation for His public ministry. He went to the desert to seek the devil, to purposefully test His readiness. Within the desert, we see the only tests and challenges that we can ever be faced with. They may ring familiar as we break them down.

First during His fast, He became hungry. This is normally when the enemy can tempt you. In the moments of hunger, when life doesn't seem to be working out for you, or in times of financial struggle, mental confusion, or emotional difficulty. But it is at this point that you are being prepared for something. You are being asked to trust and draw close to your faith.

When the devil came to Jeshua in the desert, he was there to test His resolve, as it says in Matthew 4:3–4: "Then the tempter came. 'Since you are the Son of God,' he said, 'tell these stones to become loaves of bread.'

"But He answered, 'It is written, "One must not live on bread alone, but on every word coming out of the mouth of God."'"

The first thing the enemy of your soul will always question or mock you with is your identity. In this phrase, the devil challenges Jeshua in His very understanding of being the Son of God. Jeshua, who had been present at the creation at the very beginning, had more wisdom than to challenge the very nature of physics and creation. We cannot turn stones into bread; it is against the natural order.

The enemy challenges our very security, as if the source of all creation isn't the infinite source of all abundance. Are you safe? Can you provide for yourself? As someone who has lived by faith for the last four years, I can tell you with absolute certainty: If you are walking in the aligned calling of the Higher Self, every need is supplied and sustained through Abba.

Everything I have truly needed, even if I didn't know how at the time, has been provided for. We are fully sustained as we walk with Spirit through miraculous and wonderful ways. Have a look around you and be grateful for what you have. What can you share? How have you been blessed with what is working out for you?

Watch it grow and expand. This is how we co-create our reality.

The second temptation has to do with sacred service, part of the activation pillar of the Essential Ecosystem. From Matthew 4:5–7: "Then the Devil took him to the Holy City and had him stand on the highest point of the Temple. He told Jesus, 'Since you are the Son of God, throw yourself down, because it is written, "God will put his angels in charge of you, and, with their hands they will hold you up, so that you will never hit your foot against a rock."'

"Jesus responded to him, 'It is also written, "You must not tempt the Lord your God."'"

The devil knows the scripture and uses the word of God to create confusion. We can test the divine's love for us by challenging that regardless of what we do we are protected. We need to remain in a state of grace and surrender to truly enjoy the full incorruptible protection of the Holy Spirit. We do need to remain in alignment with the seventh dimension, which is the angelic realm. (Yes—there are more than five dimensions; however, that will have to be for the next book. The mastery of the first five dimensions is our focus for now, but you can trust the angelic are in perfect alignment and always present with you.)

In the final temptation, Matthew 4:8–11: "The Devil took him to a very high mountain and showed him all the kingdoms of the world, along with their splendor. He told Jesus, 'I will give you all these things if you will bow down and worship me!'

"Then Jesus told him, 'Go away, Satan! Because it is written, "You must worship the Lord your God and serve only him."'

"So, the Devil left him, and angels came and began ministering to him."

The devil will ultimately challenge us on who we think we are because what he ultimately wants is our worship. He will give us everything we think we want. He can actually deliver every pleasure and desire of the human mind, as he is the prince of the fallen matrix, and it is a trap of the soul.

Worship is the focus of our attention, the place we put our trust or deliver our adoration. It is what we trust in and ultimately, where our soul is invested. Do we need the devil to give us the stage, the recognition, and the abundance that comes with the price of our soul? Jeshua knew better.

CHOOSING LEGACY LEADERSHIP

Happiness is peace with our own soul and conscience. It is our sovereignty. Our freedom and knowing that we are masters over our life in alignment with the source of creation.

It comes back to the idea of delivering ourselves from the idea of victimhood.

In victim mode, we may believe that we have limited choices. This is the illusion. We are infinite and abundant beings, no matter what the bank account says. No matter what the physical circumstances are. I have had a little and I have had a lot. None of it defines who I am as an infinite essence. That is up to me to decide.

And that is the source of our Christed aligned power to co-create. We are being invited to return to the Garden of Eden, the place that offers us our true spiritual inheritance. This is where we cultivate the peace, joy, love, and enlightenment of Everyday Eden in our lives and in our creations. Within the fourth dimension, I have seen that a new structure emerges for us to embrace.

Let us dive into how this understanding impacts our dimensions and the mastery we are cultivating in the different aspects of ourselves that create the whole.

Releasing the Victim/Villain Mentality
(AIR/FIRST DIMENSION/MENTAL BODY)

Instead of being a victim, we can choose to see ourselves as valiant. We are not defined by our circumstances, dear one. In truth, we are older, stronger, and deeper than just the sum of experiences we have lived through or the circumstances that may have surrounded us. We can choose to use the frequency of courage to see ourselves as valiant. No matter what we have lived through, we have survived. As I was being revealed the Ecosystem, I understood that I had never failed. I had also never been positioned to really succeed as I had never received nor given myself all the support I needed, to truly thrive.

We are survivors and by our very nature valiant.

Becoming the Victor
(WATER/SECOND DIMENSION/EMOTIONAL BODY)

Of the millions of seeds ejected into our mother's womb in the moment of conception, there was only one that penetrated (unless you are a natural twin or triplet), and that makes you a winner. One in a few million at least. A victor among victors, each and every one of us. We were chosen to incarnate into this life to find our way and our purpose in the world. To be of service and unique expression. Each one of us special by our very birthright.

When we realize the love, provision, protection, and opportunity that the very act of being alive represents, we may choose to look at life differently. This is indeed our invitation. Pride, which has been known to be the step before the fall, becomes a basis that we can rest into. Can we be proud of who we have been? Who we are? Do we trust in all that we are becoming? Would our parents be proud of us? Do we have peace with the choices we have made in our empowered state?

Accepting the Vessel
(EARTH/THIRD DIMENSION/PHYSICAL BODY)

Accepting ourselves for exactly who we are, as we are, is the beginning of abundant and eternal life. Life is happening not only to us and by us, it is happening through us. We no longer need control when we know this life to be benevolent and unconditional love.

Just as the seed in the womb didn't need to effort to grow but knew intuitively how to develop, we too can trust this life to lead and to guide. We are becoming. We don't need to rely on our cleverness. We may not be where we want to be, but we can trust that we have everything within us to become that which we most desire.

We are divinely guided on this journey. The divine alchemy in this dimension is to use and transmute our frequency of anger. Anger is something I saw in my beloved in the jungle. It is nothing more than passion that does not have permission to flow. All the places we don't trust our passion become frustrated and expressed in anger; however, with the support of alchemy, all anger becomes the unstoppable and indestructible force of passion. When we tap into this, we see the power of our creation.

Seeing Our True Value
(FIRE/FOURTH DIMENSION/ENERGETIC BODY)

As we strip the layers of illusion and separation, we heal the layers of trauma and distortion to find our true and authentic self. As we accept ourselves as enough to receive the love of our natural divinity, we find that we are truly valuable just as we are, wherever we are in our process of creation and manifestation.

As we settle in this peace, we notice that right here and now, we are worthy. What we desire, desires us. I heard this phrase many times in the spiritual community before I could truly embrace it and believe it was true. For so long, I fought for everything I owned. For so long, I experienced the deep pain of desiring something that found me undesirable, especially with Nathan. But in truth, what we desire truly desires us right back. That which is for us will never pass us by.

So, we need to hold on to our desire with all of our heart.

We need to use our consciousness, our faith, our life force to hold on to the dream that beats in rhythm with our very heartbeat. It was not easy for me to hold on to this during the last three and half years, and it may not be easy for you in this moment. Yet it is the truth. You are the very seed that will produce every manifestation in our life.

This is our co-creation. This is our legacy leadership.

THE THREE TREES

Now we return to the Garden of Eden. Each of us gets the sovereign choice to choose. Within the garden we are given three trees of which we are the incorruptible Christed seed. What do you choose, beloved?

WELCOME HOME
The Three Trees of Eden

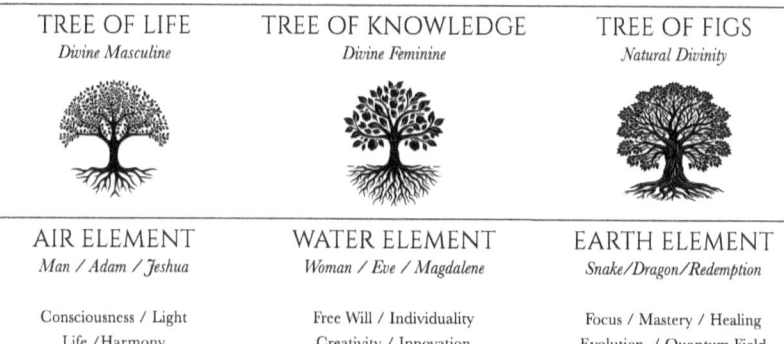

TREE OF LIFE	TREE OF KNOWLEDGE	TREE OF FIGS
Divine Masculine	*Divine Feminine*	*Natural Divinity*
AIR ELEMENT	WATER ELEMENT	EARTH ELEMENT
Man / Adam / Jeshua	Woman / Eve / Magdalene	Snake/Dragon/Redemption
Consciousness / Light	Free Will / Individuality	Focus / Mastery / Healing
Life / Harmony	Creativity / Innovation	Evolution / Quantum Field

We find the Tree of Life. The one that gives eternal life, the one in alignment with the original template and design of Genesis. The tree that longs to live once again upon this plane of planet Earth. In the jungle, I saw her. She is a tree of infinite abundance, of wisdom, communion, divine consciousness, and enlightenment. She is truly glorious and ours for the taking as we develop and embrace our natural divinity.

We have a second tree, the Tree of Knowledge, also known as the Tree of Good and Evil. Although love is truly the only thing that is real and will remain through all the passages of time, each of us has been marked with trauma, guilt, regret, and experiences when we could not tell the difference. What is good, and what is evil? That is the gift of discernment. To know what is real, good, and true is the ultimate skill of the new leadership rising and needed in this time.

No matter what we have experienced, we can make a choice to forgive our experiences. We can make the choice to learn from every moment and decide with our sovereign will to do better in the future as we move forward. We have taken the fruit—there is no turning back—yet there is an invitation to forgive and repent from the ways that have not served ourselves or our neighbor. That have not honored or elevated the divinity within us.

There is also a third tree in the garden that few ever speak of. It is the tree that has the leaves that covers our shame. It covers our nakedness as we stand in the presence of Abba, the Living God that lives within our very divinity, vibrant in our cellular structure.

This is the Fig Tree.

Shame is the lowest of frequencies and yet these leaves have the power to cover all shame, all regret, all fear. To stand once again in the presence of the almighty divine who walks with us in the cool of the day. That longs simply to hear we are here, we are willing, we are listening. Yes, we are willing to take on our mastery, our leadership, and we will remain humble students to constantly be listening and leaning in to the guidance and splendor of our higher self.

Welcome, dear one, to the Garden of Eden. The place where we as the highest authority on the face of the Earth, take a stand for peace, for unity, for humanity, for life.

This is the day that we ARISE. This is the beginning of the Age of Aquarius. The renaissance and the golden age—what all our ancestors have worked and labored for.

We are the chosen seed.

Is the choice not obvious, beloved?

May we choose wisely, as this garden is glorious and wonderful. What a shame it would be if we could not see the promise we are given.

You are the solution you have been waiting for.

You are the promise of your lineage.

The time is now. It is time to ARISE!

(YEAR OF THE SNAKE INITIATION)

Breathe in the air of a new time and space.
Welcome to your inheritance, beloved.

We honor the truth, the power, the
purity of the past, and embrace the infinite potential
of expansion and evolution
for the good, and the good, and the good,
and the right, and the true.
For all of humanity as a whole.
And only that will do. Thank you.

A declaration of independence indeed.
A shift of power from the one to the whole.
Every sacred soul of humanity is precious.
That is the only thing that is truly needing
to be understood, from our perspective.

You do not suffer alone, beloved.
We are waiting for you, too.
We are all making our way to the light.

We are all coming home.
There is no higher or lower
among Us, beloveds.

CHAPTER TWELVE
Co-Creating in the New World

I recall a particular dark and gloomy day in my relationship with Nathan where the haunting of the past and loss bore heavily on my heart. My head pulsed with words I couldn't begin to comprehend.

"Lizete—our love was not even real!" He said it like it was the most wonderful news and he couldn't wait to tell me. As if this was the news that would set us free from this toxic, twisted entanglement that suffocated our souls.

My heart shattered in a million pieces. Not real? What do you mean our love was not real? It was the realest, most visceral experience of my existence. What are you talking about? You said "I love you" twenty times a day. Every meal, every message, every concern, every effort was nothing? I was nothing? My mind scrambled.

It was in this state of confusion, walking my familiar and repetitive cycle around the neighborhood, that I connected to the inner temple space. The sanctuary within. I asked, "Abba, was it real?" I was surprised, and yet not, as the reply came as a question.

"Is time real, Lizete?"

"Yes," I answered firmly, recognizing Jeshua answering me. "Time is definitely real. Just now I was at home and now five minutes later I am here with You."

"Very good," the answer resounded. "So is time real, Lizete?"

"Definitely not." I smiled within. "It's definitely not real, as we are always in the eternal present. Right here and now, always with you in my mind." I smiled.

"Very good," came the calm and soothing affirmation of Spirit. "So how do you harmonize these two truths?"

"Well," I started, "I guess that is the biggest question I have asked myself this whole time. How do we harmonize these two truths?"

I held my breath, knowing I was opening to receive an answer to a question I had looked for my whole life. I mundanely walked my dogs and smiled at the familiar passersby.

"Time's existence is to serve and show all of the truth. All truth is known in the course of time. In the beginning was the Word, and the Word was with God. And the Word was God."

It absolutely took my breath away. In the moment it is real. We are so sure. And then life continues and in another moment in time, with additional information, invention, or new consciousness, truth appears differently. A different perspective. A higher or lower frequency.

Was the love real? For me it was and still is. It was real from that first call. It was real through the building of our home, through every argument and every incredibly tender moment. It is a love that still lives.

That love is my experience. A source nurturing me during the dungeon period of healing and restoring. Embedded in each lyric and each beat of every soul alchemy song. It was this alchemy that reached to the depths of the separation laid in stone through the eons of time. Indeed, it was love that had no end. It was love that healed me and transformed my being through ascension. It is love still that allows me to live with an open heart and access the divine field in any moment I choose. Nathan reminded me of the love I have always had access to.

And, at the same time, he had complete free will to not experience it that way. In his experience, in his truth, our love was not real.

That which is real will always be real in the length of time. The truth is but one, even though we have the perception of ours as the right one right now. Each person receives its harvest. It is all up to us. Who is worth you giving all your life force to? I would highly recommend that you use your life force to care for yourself and then extend all that you are becoming in service to others. Creating value for self and others is the new template.

We only need to love without attachment to outcome.

This revelation informed the way I now lead the ARISE Academy. Each person is met as a master of their journey as well as a student of the infinite way. We focus only on reconnecting each person to their very own individual, perfect, higher self. The nature, look, and feel of love is interpreted in every age, in every race, and every moment in time as a singular universal vibration.

The master of our unique expression in this frequency is the medicine for both self and the whole. Each of us, as a piece of the puzzle, are empowered to embody the natural divinity we are, and to take our unique place in the whole.

This is the vision I carry for the evolution of the ARISE Academy, which was channeled and penned in 2022, right at the beginning of the healing journey that has led me to this book. I now lovingly gift it to you.

Though I don't know what is going on in your life, I understand that there is pressure, no doubt. Believe me, I know. As I pen these words, I have bills coming in. I have rent due. I have animals that I'm responsible for and a future that is unwritten and unscripted. Things are not exactly where I want them to be either. The good news is that we get to accept the responsibility of writing the next chapter.

And, in many cases, a whole new book.

In truth, there are loves that never end. There are moments that we want to capture forever and hope will never leave. These are glimpses of our truest and most natural state of being, moments of pure love. We don't get to control when it happens. We only get to choose to be it. Right now.

Now, in this moment of infinite possibility, we can welcome the same frequency to meet us where we are. Co-creating in this whole new world is not for that faint of heart. But we are not that, are we, dear one? We are made of the toughest material in existence.

We are made in the image of God itself.

We are not the totality of Abba (Mother and Father God), of course, but we are sons and daughters. For this reason, and no matter the circumstance, I hope our journey together has inspired you with great hope. The answer is truly within you, right here and now.

As a guide and a fellow human being, I will never tell people what to believe, what to think, or how to feel about anything, for that is truly our individual prerogative. The universe has nothing but time.

Before I began writing this work, Spirit called me to fast for seven days and seven nights.

These three guidelines, these fundamental principles, for the curriculum emerged:

- **Awareness (Sovereignty):** Humanity awakened to the regenerative power and abundance of the planet.

- **Activation (Sacred Service):** Reconnected to the benevolence of their own natural divine consciousness.

- **Alignment (Security):** Free to express and explore their sacred soul gifts and co-create their unique Everyday Eden.

This is the core of the Essential Ecosystem. Each of our unique contributions and creations creates a place for ourselves in the world and a better world for the whole. There is no paradox, dogma, nor domination required. The only condition is we don't get to control anyone else but ourselves.

We get to accept the other's truth, experience, and journey. We get to love and we get to let go. We get to accept that although we are naturally divine, we are also hurt, traumatized, and each on our own journey of finding our way home. We get to choose to love every person that comes along the path, no matter their form. We also get to be grateful for those who we learn to say no to and stop at the door.

We are each reclaiming the balance of our love and our power.

Each of us has lived our own unique story and writes it even now. I hope that this book, the work of the ARISE Academy, and every soul alchemy song I ever sing, help others find the way to peace. I hope to share this roadmap through the maze as I have been shown it. The way you navigate your journey is completely always up to you. I hope this is an exciting idea for you, beloved.

There is so much of life that is yet to be lived.

Jeremiah 29:11: "'For I know the plans I have for you,' declares the Lord, 'plans to prosper you and not to harm you, plans to give you hope and a future.'"

Once we know within ourselves that divinity is real, that God and love and all that is sacred are the most real things there are, we begin a new level of the journey. Love wants us to live in alignment with our soul and create abundance from that. The energetic realm, or the element of fire, is the unseen and powerful force of transmutation and multidimensionality. We master this to stabilize and utilize this innate human potential, guided by the beautiful power of faith. And faith is essential in our journey.

Hebrews 11:6: "Now without faith it is impossible to please God, for whoever comes to him must believe that he exists and that he rewards those who diligently search for him."

Faith is being able to see what is not yet manifest, but that which is intended. Not by putting a laundry list on the divine, but to tune in, akin to using a compass that will always point true north. It is important to have a trustworthy navigation system as we traverse the known, the unknown, and the unknowable in each moment of our journey. It is about accepting where we are and trusting in the next step as a necessary part. I promise you that your higher self will never set you up. Only our conditioning would ever do that.

Being able to distinguish between the truth and our conditioning is our whole objective on the journey to wholeness. This was truly the difference I always found in religious leaders versus truly awakened and conscious co-creators. The former uses their faith to hope and pray that a God exists. The latter uses faith to take each step into the unknowable with courage and a clear conscience. They choose with each step to know and to trust the truth within, regardless of outward appearance.

We are not here to survive, dear one, as we are indeed eternal. We are here to surrender and co-create with this incredible life force we know as love.

The process of faith I have found is the multidimensional understanding I have experienced through the different elements. The simple construct that came to me is a point of focus for each of these levels of consciousness.

This approach will hopefully serve you well as a simple memorable framework to calibrate yourself effectively whenever you need it.

CO-CREATING IN THE NEW WORLD
Moving Toward Wholeness

Masculine Polarity — **Feminine Polarity**

AIR ELEMENT
Mental Body
First Dimension
Gratitude

SPACE ELEMENT
Light Body
Fifth Dimension
Grace

WATER ELEMENT
Emotional Body
Second Dimension
Gentleness

FIRE ELEMENT
Energetic Body
Fourth Dimension
Growth

EARTH ELEMENT
Physcial Body
Third Dimension
Grit

Gratitude
(AIR/FIRST DIMENSION/MENTAL BODY)

The focus of gratitude supports us to focus on the abundance, provision, and sustenance that is in our current creation. It is the most natural state that we can consciously choose that unlocks the highest of frequencies, for the mental body: peace, joy, and love. When we set our focus on appreciation for all circumstances, we start to train our mind in that direction. Our perspective is everything, and there is a reason we have learned so much on gratitude.

Gentleness
(WATER/SECOND DIMENSION/EMOTIONAL BODY)

For a long time, I was convinced that kindness was the ideal state for the emotional body, while through the Essential Ecosystem I clearly learned that there is nothing I can give another that is not first cultivated within myself. For me to be loving and kind and in alignment with the mental body, I need to cultivate a state of gentleness within myself. In the forgiving and gentle awareness of self, we can then cultivate this gentleness to extend to others as a natural byproduct.

This is why at ARISE Academy, we teach using guided transcendental meditation as well as theory. An easy way to be mindful of this is to understand the ocean. The ocean offers inevitable high and low tides, but as we purify and release unconscious trauma and alchemize into higher frequency energy, the water becomes calmer. We continue to feel everything but have mastery not to react to those that simply want a rise out of us. Gentleness also cultivates the divine frequencies of reason, acceptance, willingness, and neutrality.

Grit
(EARTH/THIRD DIMENSION/PHYSICAL BODY)

Determination to hold on to the dream as we take our cycles and pathways up and down the mountain of life's highways takes about the most courageous grit that exists. But it is also the only thing that makes dreams happen. The only thing that can ever stop your potential from blossoming is your decision to conform to a situation that is not up to the standard of what you know in your heart is really right for you. We need to live with an open heart, feeling the pain and loss of what is not there, so we can have the courage to alchemize that reality into the manifest that is in alignment with our essence.

The initial words I channeled in 2019 in the jungle were: "A seed if left on barren ground will never produce the fruit it is innately born to give." This is the inspiration. This Ecosystem supports me to navigate time and space, and how to best utilize the aspects of courage, pride, anger, and desire, which are the major frequencies that cause us to react or to create. An evolved ego, perhaps.

What do I want? Am I being true to that desire? Hard but necessary questions. When our desire is not able to flow, it causes anger. If I would change anything in the Hawkins Map of Consciousness, it would be to change "anger" to "passion."

Once our desire is aligned, our passion is free to flow. Anger normally only exists due to pent-up energy. When we move in passion and are free, our wounds of anger are no more. Alchemy.

Our pride in ourselves comes naturally when we are loved and appreciated for who we are. If our mothers and fathers are proud of the people we have become, if our community values our presence and contribution, pride no longer becomes a stumbling block before the fall. We are not being anything but ourselves. That is the highest we can all truly be, and only we—in each and every heart—can judge if we have measured up to the potential within.

It takes true grit to know ourselves and to love ourselves and go for what we truly desire. Especially when the people we most love don't seem to want us to have that or fight us at every step. With the cultivation of the mental and water elements, our journey is more equipped to support us to navigate in harmony.

Growth
(FIRE/FOURTH DIMENSION/ENERGETIC BODY)

The unseen realm—where the densest and most difficult frequencies have been stored in our DNA and unconscious memory banks—is where we experience growth. Realizing that nothing was wrong with me gave me the alignment and use of the fire to purify all grief, apathy, guilt, and shame. This is how we truly drain the swamp.

Each person has had their burden and cross to bear, their own life lived in the lower matrix. Each person has been hurt in some way. Everywhere this pain lives is part of our evolutionary journey to heal and restore. With the tools of alchemy, we can take these inherited and inherent pieces of lead and transform them into pure gold. We can see every hardship as something that makes us a stronger, better, and more compassionate human being.

This is a win for the soul. This is a win for the whole.

This is how we are one.

Grace
(SPACE, FIFTH DIMENSION, SOUL BODY)

Each step of the journey, we can choose to wake up every morning with the full intention of having a good day. When we can keep this understanding and reverence that each soul is walking on their journey with God, we can embrace that indeed, we only live by grace. The grace we give ourselves is the grace we grant others. The infinite love that holds us all. We take nothing for granted, and this is the space where enlightenment and true empowerment lives.

Grace is renewed every morning. It's free energy!

This is the gift. This is the invitation. I personally call this the energy of Everyday Eden. It is the promise, and now she beckons us home.

Can woman have it all? That is the quest and that is the question. Everything I have experienced in this journey, beloved, tells me that the answer is within us.

WELCOME HOME

The evolution continues, and I am honored that you have journeyed with me. May we become all that we were meant to be. For ourselves, for our lover, for our community, family, and friends. For the generations that will come after us.

This is an invitation to peace, to return to the garden, and I am so excited to meet you there.

RESOURCES

Free Masterclass
Within this free ninety-minute masterclass, I break down in detail how the different parts of ourselves can be harmonized. Sign up today at
lizetemorais.com/masterclass

Free Resources on the ARISE Website
On the ARISE Academy website, **ariseacademy.co,** I have a free resources page including many different introductory courses, free uplifting meditations, and life-transforming transmissions.

RECOMMENDED READING

Along my journey, many books were shared with me that confirmed, validated, and mirrored the understandings and revelations I've shared with you in this book. I have not referenced these works, nor am I affiliated with their authors, but each of them helped me enormously. I hope they can also be of support to you as you continue your journey into Everyday Eden.

- *Accessing Your Multidimensional Self: A Key to Cosmic History* by Stephanie South

- *Book of the Timespace: Cosmic History Chronicles Volume V, Time and Society: Envisioning the New Earth, The Relative Aspiring to the Absolute* by Jose Arguelles and Stephanie South

- *The Crystalline Transmission: A Synthesis of Light* (The Crystal Trilogy Vol. 3) by Katarina Raphaell

- *The Holy Bible* (any translation)

- *The Magdalen Manuscript: The Alchemies of Horus & the Sex Magic of Isis* by Tom Kenyon and Judi Sion

- *The New Wine Is Better: The Story of One Man Who Saw the Invisible, Believed the Incredible, and Received the Impossible* by Robert Thom

- *Women Who Run with the Wolves: Myths and Stories of the Wild Woman Archetype* by Clarissa Pinkola Estés

ACKNOWLEDGMENTS

There are so many people to thank, but this book would not be complete without a few mentions for some critical individuals that have made all the difference.

Firstly I am grateful to God—Abba—Jeshua—Divine for this life. All of it—the good, bad and the ugly—as I see the weaving of the perfection that brought me here and now. Finally building at peace, that there is a loving benevolent intelligence in charge that I get to co-create with. I feel I get to breathe for the first time, and indeed fly higher than I ever dreamed possible. Eternally grateful for your wisdom, guidance and protection at all times at each step of the journey.

Mom and Dad, you are truly my best friends and I am grateful for your unconditional love and your ever-present dedication. You taught me devotion, through the good and easy as well as the tough times. Thank you for your love and for my life. I am eternally grateful.

To my sister Cidalia, her husband Edson and my nephew Gabriel: thank you for being family and reminding me every day what is most sacred and worth everything to create a life of legacy.

To him I have called Nathan: losing you allowed me to find my true self and my voice. You showed me how I gave myself away and confused love with sacrifice. I am grateful for each step and wish you every blessing in your onward journey.

To my business partner, soul sister, and greatest support Valerie White: there are truly no words to thank you for the faith, trust and unconditional dedication you have given to me and to the ARISE Academy. I am so excited about building the future with you side by side.

To the ARISE Collective, those past and current: you have been the most validating, encouraging and most loving souls that have supported me to spread my wings and to lead in a new way. Watching you transform, develop, grow and shine is my greatest joy and professional fulfillment. It is an honor to walk with you.

To my publisher Bryna Haynes: your excellence, example, and expert support has made what seemed impossible to me, possible. You have served in so many ways as a mentor, friend, and an exemplary woman leader dedicated to peace and the prosperity of our human collective and planet. Thank you for your endless patience and your kindness that created the cocoon for this project to be birthed. You are incredible, and I am honored and beyond blessed to have you in my corner.

To my editor Audra Figgins: thank you for your genius, and for seeing where I needed to add, deepen, soften, and erase to make this story what it is today. You challenged, encouraged, and expanded this manuscript into a book that I know I will treasure for the rest of my life, and hope that many others will treasure as well.

To every person mentioned in this book. Nathan, Maren, Carole, Sally, Paula, Angela and Varvara to mention a few ... All of you have been my creative partners in this work. I am grateful for each and every one of you. You taught me how to walk in the calling that I now follow. May you each flourish into the souls you were born to be, and fulfill your highest calling and potential. Thank you for being part of my journey to ARISE.

ABOUT THE AUTHOR

Lizete Morais retired from her corporate executive role at age thirty-five, turning into a cosmic consciousness author, Love mediumship mentor and teacher of inner ancient alchemy.

She has used her natural sacred and multi-dimensional gifts since 2012 to serve leaders, guardians, lovers, and creatives, co-create the next step in their unique Everyday Eden with Crystalline Clarity.

Her favorite ways to serve in this sacred work is life changing nature immersions, sacred ceremonies of holographic sound, long term mentoring on the evolutionary journey, and online experiences that support you to unravel the core paradox. For each, the journey will be different, unique, and universal.

All is serving one thing! Solving the paradox that sits between you and your natural divine connection to your self-healing and sovereignty, ARISE is her legacy in service to yours. Activating our Natural Divinity is our own personal soul's evolution revealed. That is all we need to create our unique Everyday Eden.

Learn more about Lizete, download the ARISE app, and access free resources at **ariseacademy.co** and **lizetemorais.com**.

ABOUT THE PUBLISHER

Founded in 2021 by Bryna Haynes, WorldChangers Media is a boutique publishing company focused on "Ideas for Impact." We know that great books change lives, topple outdated paradigms, and build movements. Our commitment is to deliver superior-quality transformational nonfiction by, and for, the next generation of thought leaders.

Ready to write and publish your thought leadership book? Learn more at **worldchangers.media**.

www.ingramcontent.com/pod-product-compliance
Lightning Source LLC
Chambersburg PA
CBHW022052160426
43198CB00008B/202